3-9-76

BARELY AUDIBLE

A HISTORY OF THE DENVER BRONCOS

by Larry Gordon and Dick Burnell

Graphic Impressions, Inc./publisher
Denver, Colorado – 1975

Special appreciation is expressed to the Denver Bronco football organization for its cooperation and support and for its willingness to provide information and interviews regarding the Denver Bronco team, individual players, and the history of the organization. In addition, grateful acknowledgment is made to the following for their contributions to this book: To Cheryl Meyer for layout and design; to AlphaGraphics, especially Paul Schmidt and Barbara Korpi, Hoflund Graphics, and Graphic Impressions for composition and internal graphics; to Lucien Berrier and Bradford Printing; to Dick Burnell, Frank Grill, Ken Bloom, Larry Sampson, Fred Dumke and Gary Gruisinger of Photo Associates for pictures; to William Davis for color separations. Jacket design by Graphic Impressions.

Acknowledgment is also made to the following, who have graciously given permission to reprint material from their publications: the Chicago Tribune, excerpts from Denver's Dirty Tricks Backfire, *by Don Pierson; The Cincinnati Enquirer, excerpts from* Nightmare in Denver, *by Dick Forbes; The Dallas Morning News, excerpts from* Cowboy Defense Turns Denver Over *and* Bundle of Mistakes, *by Bob St. John; The Denver Post, excerpts made available through the courtesy of Charles R. Buxton, editor and publisher of The Denver Post, Inc.; The Houston Post, excerpts from* Broncos Bash Oilers, *by David Casstevens, © 1973 The Houston Post Co.; The Kansas City Times, excerpts from* Chiefs Stymie Broncos *and* Chiefs Last Gasp Falls A Bobble Short, *by Bill Richardson, The Kansas City Star Co.; excerpts from the Los Angeles Herald Examiner by Melvin Durslag; the Mayfield Publishing Co. (formerly National Press Books), excerpts from* Coaching Today's Athlete, *by John Ralston, Mike White with Stanley Wilson, © 1973 John Ralston, Mike White, and Stanley Wilson; The New York Times, excerpts from* Broncos Down Jets on First-Half Surge, *by Murray Chase, © 1973 The New York Times Co.; the Oakland Tribune, excerpts from* Raiders Let Win Slip Away, *by Tom LaMarre, and* Raiders Sniffed Ralston's Bowl Gadget, *by Bob Valli, © 1973 The Tribune Publishing Co.; the Pittsburgh Post-Gazette, excerpt from* Steelers Can't Bust Broncos, *by Jack Sell; Playboy Magazine, excerpts; Playboy Press, excerpt from* Cosell, *by Howard Cosell, © 1973 Playboy Enterprises, Inc.; Random House, Inc., excerpts from* Always on the Run, *by Larry Csonka, Jim Klick with Dave Anderson, © 1973 Random House, Inc.; the St. Louis Post-Dispatch, excerpts from* Denver TD Plan Foiled by Late Big Red Stand, *by Tom Barnidge, The San Diego Union, excerpts from* Broncos Spoil Bid by Waller, *by Jerry Magee, and* Chargers No Bronco Busters, *by Chuck Sawyer, reprinted by courtesy of the Union-Tribune Publishing Co.; the San Francisco Chronicle, excerpts from* Gossett Saves 49ers, *by Darrell Wilson, © 1973, Chronicle Publishing Co.; The Saturday Evening Post, excerpt by Myron Cope, © 1973 The Curtis Publishing Co.; Sportscope, excerpts through the courtesy of Sam Lusky, Publisher; and Sports Illustrated, excerpts from articles by Robert Boyle, Tex Maule, Joe Marshall, Edwin Shrake, through the courtesy of the publisher, Time Inc.*

CONTENTS

THE
WAY WE
WERE

History's patch-
works are sewn
with fragile threads
of coincidence.
A broken or
misplaced strand
along the way
might have meant
the San Antonio
Broncos, the
Atlanta Broncos,
or no Broncos at
all. Denver's
development of
a durable pro-
fessional franchise
is a unique
combination of
events initially
unrelated to
football; a series
of seemingly
serious setbacks
that worked out
for the best; and
the efforts of some
dedicated,
persistent people.
This is the story
of those events,
setbacks and
people...

The 24-year-old National Football League had already shot down three satellite leagues by 1946 when the All-American Football Conference appeared. After four seasons, three AFC teams—Baltimore, Cleveland and San Francisco—managed to infiltrate the senior league. The other AFC teams disbanded, placing their players in a draft pool. The new 1950 NFL alignment, two six-team conferences, remained intact for almost two decades.

In 1947, before the AFC's sophomore season, football history started in Denver with baseball. Will Nicholson and good friend Eddie Nicholson brought the Bears out of hibernation and installed them in shabby, rundown Merchants Park. The Nicholsons hired a local construction firm to give the Broadway Street eyesore a facelift.

Lamar Hunt conferring with Denver's Cal Kunz.

"It was a horrible place to play ball," recalled Gerry Phipps. "The stands were awful. We repaired and painted them. The press box was a safety hazard, up on a rickety roof. We moved it behind home plate, but after we rebuilt the dished infield, the reporters' eyes were just above field level. There was no grass on the infield and no sod farms in those days. My Dad had a house near Denver University. I took grass from the corner of his lawn and planted it in the infield."

"The lighting was terrible," Phipps continued. "One night some big Bears outfielder—I forget his name—put an extra ball in his pocket. You could hardly see what was going on in the outfield so when somebody hit one out of the park, this guy took out the ball, banged it against the metal-plated fence, picked it up and threw the batter out at second base. It was one of the funniest things I ever saw."

After repairing Merchants Park, Phipps bought stock in Rocky Mountain Empire Sports, Inc., and accepted an offer to serve on its board of directors. When the Howsams bought the Bears in 1948, Phipps remained on the board and his construction company converted a garbage dump into beautiful Bears Stadium. Financing the new ballpark fell about $60,000 short but Phipps was repaid in full after the Bears' first season. A few years later the Bears were winning Pacific Coast championships and setting minor league attendance records.

It was a pleasant way to spend a summer evening," said Phipps, a baseball fan since he was old enough to read the scores. "People brought picnic baskets out to the game and had themselves a good time."

While the Bears steadily gained popularity in the fifties, pro football slowly started challenging its more relaxed rival for the mythical "national pastimeship." Increasing annual profits prompted a few businessmen around the country to seek a piece of the action. One such man was Texas millionaire Lamar Hunt, who tried either to buy an existing team or secure an expansion franchise for Dallas.

Unable to gain entrée into the NFL by either route, Hunt and Houston's Bud Adams decided to create a new league. On August 14, 1959, Hunt, Adams, New York's Harry Wismer, Los Angeles' Barron Hilton, Minneapolis' Max Winter and Denver baseball boss Bob Howsam met in Chicago and formed the American Football League.

"It took us completely by surprise," said Phipps. "We had talked about getting more use out of Bears Stadium, but nobody even mentioned football. Howsam came back from Chicago with facts and figures. He said we could swing it for around $400,000. It sounded crazy, but we went ahead anyway."

Boston and Buffalo joined the six original AFL members. Minneapolis, besieged by stadium problems, was replaced by Oakland. Two four-team divisions were formed—Boston, Buffalo, Houston and New York in the East and Dallas, Denver, Los Angeles and Oakland in the West. Joe Foss, a Marine fighter pilot and former South Dakota governor was appointed league commissioner.

In one of his first official statements, Foss told reporters, "The AFL was formed because men in certain communities felt a need to respond to public demands. When repeated bids for pro franchises were rejected without tangible encouragement, this group decided that the lone course available was formation of a second league."

The immediate future of the "second league" was secured by a multi-year pact with ABC-TV. The contract involved far less money than CBS was paying the NFL, but the added income helped the AFL offset some operating expenses and gave the toddling league needed national exposure. With wide-open, offense-oriented football and two substantial sponsors, Gillette and Chrysler, the AFL forced its way into American living rooms.

Gillette gave up on the AFL, but Chrysler kept the faith. Dick Forbes, a Chrysler advertising executive, told *Sports Illustrated,* "It was embarrassing for us to be associated with the AFL in some of those awful early games. But we had the guts to stay with it. The owners were young and wealthy. It was just a matter of time."

In their first two seasons the Broncos participated in several of those "awful early games." The Howsams had hired Dean Griffing as general manager and Frank Filchock to be Denver's first head coach.

Frank Filchock

Filchock spent almost 25 years in professional football. After setting passing records at Indiana University, he joined the Redskins in 1938. In 1940 Frank's fumble on his own two led to one of the Bears' 11 touchdowns as Chicago "edged" Washington 73-0 for the NFL title.

Five years later Filchock replaced injured Redskin star Sammy Baugh in the championship game against Cleveland. Throwing in windy, sub-zero weather, Baugh had earlier hit his own goal posts with an errant pass for what was an automatic safety and two points in those days. Filchock came in and threw two TD passes, but Washington lost 15-14.

As a passing halfback for the 1946 New York Giants, Filchock was implicated in a gambling scandal with teammate Merle Hapes. Prior to the Bears-Giants title tilt both were questioned about their failure to report a bribery attempt. Hapes was suspended immediately. Filchock was permitted to play. His two touchdown tosses provided all the Giants' scoring as the Bears won 24-14. After the game Filchock was banned from the NFL.

Frank went to Canada. As a player and coach there his teams appeared in eight playoff games. He was named Canadian Player of 1949 after helping Montreal win the Grey Cup. The NFL lifted Filchock's suspension in 1950. He played briefly for Baltimore before returning to Canada where he helped Dean Griffing build Regina into a CFL power.

Dean Griffing

When they both moved to Denver, Griffing immediately established a reputation for thrift, reportedly recovering footballs kicked into the stands at home games. "Dean was so tight," one former player commented, "you had to prove your shoestrings were broken before you could get a new pair."

Griffing's most famous money-saving move was the purchase of "compromise" uniforms, a single set of yellow jerseys and drab brown pants that could be worn at both home and away games. The bargain-minded Bronco GM supposedly bought the grotesque garb from Tucson's defunct Copper Bowl. With the addition of vertical striped socks, the Broncos led the league in ugly uniforms.

They also led the Western Division after four games in 1960. After losing all five pre-season games, Denver became the first AFL team to win an official game when they beat Lou Saban's 16-point favorite Patriots 13-10 in Boston. The Broncos scored on a 59-yard swing pass from Frank Tripucka to Al Carmichael in the second quarter. Gene Mingo, who rushed for 66 yards in eight carries, set up another score when he returned Tom Greene's punt 74 yards in the third period. Safety Goose Gonsoulin preserved the historic victory with an interception on the Bronco two-yard line at the end of the game.

Three weeks later, in Denver's first home game, the Broncos busted Oakland 31-14. Lionel Taylor caught seven passes, two for touchdowns, to give the locals a 3-1 record and first place in the West. After eight games the Broncos were 4-4. Overall, they have never been near .500 since. Denver's 13-year string of losing seasons includes a curious trend that seems to strike the Broncos in the second half of every season. In their first 12 years Denver won just 14 of 84 second-half games. In the last half of 1960 the Broncos were 0-6-1.

In both halves of 1960 Empire Sports lost $200,000, forcing Bob Howsam to try to unload the unprofitable operation. He found an interested San Antonio syndicate, but before the Bears and Broncos departed for Texas, a group headed by Calvin Kunz, Jr., bought Howsam's holdings. On June 1, 1961, a week after the sale, Kunz was placed in charge of Empire Sports.

Gerry Phipps became the largest single stockholder with the shares he acquired in the Kunz-Howsam deal. "I always liked having baseball in Denver," said Phipps. "At first it really did not matter to me whether we had pro football or not. But once the Broncos were here, I wanted to help keep them. Nothing looks worse to the rest of the country than a growing community losing its professional sports franchise."

During the 1961 campaign Kunz became very involved in Bronco operations. Some players in that era thought he was too involved and objected to his constant suggestions concerning what plays to run, who to play where, and how to win more ball games. "He meddled," said one ex-Bronco, "and it hurt us a lot more than it helped."

The Broncos posted a 3-11 record in 1961, losing all of their last seven games. Filchock was released and replaced by young, energetic Jack Faulkner. The 34-year-old head coach also became general manager when Griffing was fired. Faulkner fattened up his coaching staff by bringing Mac Speedie, Jack Martin, Gary Glick and Ray Malavasi into the Bronco corral.

Coaches generally approach a new assignment with enthusiasm and overt optimism. Jovial Jack Faulkner was no exception. After arriving in Denver he made hundreds of public appearances to assure Bronco fans they would be supporting a winner in 1962. He was almost right.

Faulkner, an ex-Marine, earned letters in track, baseball and football at Ohio's Miami University. Sid Gillman was Jack's football coach at Miami before Gillman went to the University of Cincinnati. After college, as a scout for Cleveland, Faulkner once submitted this report: "I have seen him play several

times. I think he's tough. You may not be interested in him, but I think he's a good one." The Browns rejected the recommendation for John Unitas.

After scouting for Cleveland, Jack joined Sid Gillman's staff at Cincinnati. Together they moved to the Los Angeles Rams, then to the Los Angeles and San Diego Chargers. It was a 14-year friendship and learning experience for Faulkner. He rewarded his old coach by helping Denver defeat San Diego in both 1962 meetings.

Earl Hartman — Bronco's Business Manager from 1962-1972. An annual Earl F. Hartman Memorial Award is now presented to Denver's top offensive and defensive players.

Some football followers believe the new NFL Cowboys pushed Hunt's Texans out of Dallas. "Not true," said Gerry Phipps. "The Texans actually had higher attendance figures when both teams were there. Lamar just got a better offer from Kansas City."

NFL attempts to intimidate the new league in the early sixties spawned a $10 million anti-trust suit. In 1962 U.S. District Court Judge Roscel Thomsen ruled against the AFL action charging the NFL with monopoly and conspiracy in areas of expansion, television and player signings. A year later the U.S. Fourth Circuit Court of Appeals upheld Thomsen's decision, ending three years of litigation between the leagues.

Before Boyle's article the Broncos had turned a corner of their own. Prior to the 1962 pre-season Jack Faulkner conducted a ceremonial burning of the Broncos' fancy footwear. On August 24 the "new-look" Broncos won one of the most important games in their brief history.

Riding a nine-game losing streak—the last seven 1961 games and the first two pre-season outings—the Broncos trailed Dallas 24-17 with less than five minutes to play. The Texans, faced with fourth-and-one on Denver's 29, went for the first down. The Broncos held; tied the game with a touchdown; and won it with a field goal in overtime.

By 1962 the AFL was more than a passing fancy. *Sports Illustrated's* prognosticator, Tex Maule, had written in 1960, "The AFL will survive for two years. By then, the NFL may be willing to accept the strongest of the AFL survivors, in which case Lamar Hunt, who only wanted a pro club for Dallas in the first place, will have accomplished his purpose."

The predicted two years passed with only one AFL casualty. Harry Wismer's New York Titans went bankrupt. The league assumed financial responsibility for the team until Sonny Werblin bought and renamed them the Jets. Hunt's Dallas Texans became the Kansas City Chiefs. Hunt explained a few years later, "I quite honestly wanted to keep my franchise in Dallas. But the Kansas City people just made things so attractive we had to accept their offer. I have had no reason to regret the move."

The courtroom loss did not delay the AFL's emergence as a pro football reality. In 1962 *Sports Illustrated* writer Robert Boyle conceded, "The league has turned the corner. Any number of AFL players would do well in the NFL," citing Denver's Lionel Taylor as an example. "In two good draft years," Boyle admitted, "the AFL should be close to matching the NFL."

The Broncos beat Oakland in their final exhibition game and returned to Denver in high spirits. Fan support reached new altitudes. Ex-pro pitcher Mark Freeman formed the Quarterback Club and other pro-Bronco organizations developed. The Broncos responded with a 31-21 opening day victory over San Diego before an SRO crowd at DU Stadium.

Denver rolled through the first half of the season with an impressive 6-1 record. Second-half sickness struck again as the Broncos dropped six of their last seven games and finished the year in second place with a 7-7 record. Players on that team attribute their turnaround to two factors—defensive deterioration and Faulkner's changing coaching technique.

Offensive guard Bob McCullough said, "Our weak defense got weaker. We did not surprise anyone the second time we played them. We were 7-3 when we played Dallas for the division lead. They beat us 24-3 in Denver. The next week New York beat us here 46-45. When you score 45 points, you should win the game. After that, we were out of it."

"Faulkner was loose and easy at the beginning, fun to play for," said All-AFL lineman Jerry Sturm. "Then he started changing things, making it all more complicated. We started the season with 40 or 50 offensive plays and very basic defenses. By the sixth or seventh game we were trying to run about 150 different plays. I think the pressure of being on top got to him."

Faulkner's runnerup finish earned him Coach of the Year honors. Hoping to better the Broncos' break-even record he hired two new coaches, Red Miller and Ed Hughes. TCU graduate Allen Hurst left Houston to become Denver's trainer—a position he still holds. The future looked bright for 1963.

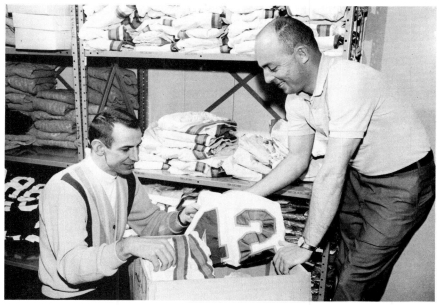

Allen Hurst and Equipment Manager Larry Elliott prepare spare Bronco uniforms for shipment to Vietnam.

On July 18 the Broncos beat Houston 17-14 with more than 6,000 Colorado Springs fans watching history's first all-rookie pro game. In August Charlie Mitchell, Tom Janik and Tom Nomina were the first future Broncos to play in Chicago's College All-Star game. Promising newcomers Mickey Slaughter, Billy Joe, Willie Brown and Hewritt Dixon were expected to bolster the Broncos.

Despite their semi-successful 1962 season and a bumper crop of good-looking rookies, Denver won only two games in 1963—none in the last half of the season. Lionel Taylor captured the AFL receiving crown for the fourth straight year. Billy Joe was named Rookie of the Year. Goose Gonsoulin was the lone Bronco to make the AFL All-Star team. After the season Denver participated in a nine-player trade, sending Gene Prebola, Wahoo McDaniel, Gordy Holz and Bob Zeman to New York for Dick Guesman, Ed Cooke, Jim Price, Sid Fournet and Charlie Janerette.

Later in January 1964, with local football fires barely burning, the future of the American Football League exploded into bright flames.

The AFL signed a lucrative, five-year pact with NBC-TV. Pete Rozelle was partially responsible for perpetuating the new league.

The NBC-AFL agreement followed a flurry of cloak-and-dagger activity between the commissioner and television. Rozelle requested sealed bids from ABC, CBS and NBC, threatening at one point to form his own NFL network if TV balked at submitting secret proposals. CBS, with hints of inter-network intrigue, narrowly bettered NBC's bid to telecast NFL games. So NBC decided to spend the money on the AFL. Joe Foss said it all, "People have now stopped asking me if we are going to make it."

Carl Lindemann, then vice-president of NBC Sports, signed the $36 million deal. Lindemann explained why to a leading sports publication:

"We knew the men operating the AFL were sportsmen of financial means. The courage they showed in the face of great odds in starting the AFL was proof of their dedication to pro football . . .

"The AFC succumbed after four years of operation, but in looking to the past we realized that one very important factor makes equating the AFL and AFC useless. That factor is television. Football games were not televised in the 1946-49 era of the AFC. Therefore, the struggling league was not able to get the national exposure—nor the residual financial benefits—television affords today . . .

"We were not interested in merely presenting the AFL games on television, but were interested in seeing that the AFL's status was enhanced and with equally important long-range benefits."

The commissioner's sealed-bid strategy was only one plateau on his continuing climb to reap more financial rewards for the NFL. When Rozelle took office in 1960 he convinced NFL owners that by representing all the teams he could give the league more power in negotiating television contracts. Rozelle was right. *Playboy* interviewer Lawrence Linderman labels the commissioner, "the most powerful sports czar of the century," pointing out that in Pete's first year the 12 NFL teams were averaging about $75,000 each. In 1973, 26 teams shared a TV jackpot worth more than $45 million.

The marriage of football and television was not made in Heaven. TV's total investment in sports was zero until 1939, when part of a Columbia-Princeton baseball game was telecast. Today's TV sports budgets are estimated at $150 million and increasing annually. Each year's programming includes more games, a wider variety of technical innovations, added commentators and analysts. ABC's Roone Arledge

has publicly suggested sports has passed the point of no return.

"So many sports organizations," said the producer, "have built their entire budgets around television that if we ever withdrew the money, the whole structure would just collapse."

En route to becoming sports primary source of financial support, television has produced revolutionary and irrevocable changes in the game. The untimely TV time-out, strange starting times, and the classic *Heidi*-interrupted Jets-Raiders game are mild examples of television's interference. The influence of TV was vividly illustrated in the first Super Bowl. Trailing 14-10 Kansas City received to start the second half. When Green Bay kicked off, NBC was doing a commercial. With instant replays not yet perfected, the Packers actually had to kick off again. One wonders what NBC directors would have done if the Chiefs scored a touchdown on the first, unseen kickoff.

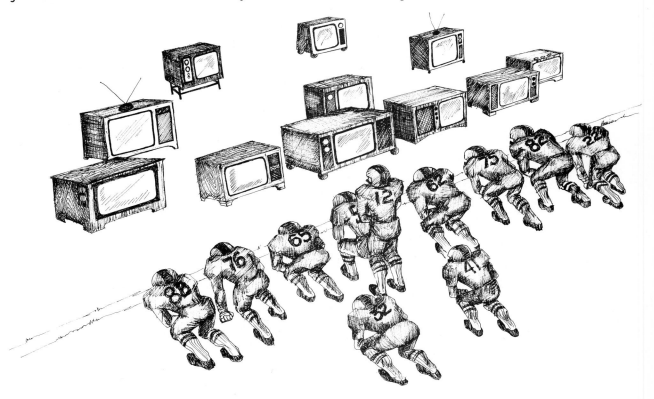

Football folks tolerate the interference. Bear Bryant once said, "We think TV exposure is so important to this university (Alabama) that we schedule ourselves to fit the medium. I'll play at midnight if that's what TV wants."

At first opposed to television's increasing influence, Vince Lombardi finally admitted to newsmen, "We do have to put forth some cooperation with television. If they ask us to start a little later so more people can see the game, we have to cooperate somewhat. Given today's budgets, there would not be a single franchise left in the NFL without television."

Commenting on the AFL-NBC contract Gerry Phipps said, "I thought it would help us significantly. They were even going to give us an advance so we could sign high draft choices. We drafted Dick Butkus, but could not sign him."

"As it turned out," Phipps told sportswriter Dick Connor, "if we had succeeded in signing some of the players we almost signed, for the terms we proposed, we probably would not have made it through the 1965 season.

There was almost no 1965 football season in Denver anyway. The Broncos lost their first four games in 1964. Mac Speedie replaced the fallen Jack Faulkner. Speedie was a superb receiver everywhere he played— high school and college in Utah, the Army Air Corps, the AFC, the National and Canadian Football Leagues.

Mac Speedie led the All-American Conference in receiving with 201 catches for 3554 yards and 24 touchdowns in four years.

Speedie's term began on October 5, 1964. Mac was the first Bronco head coach to open practices to the public. He believed fan support was an essential element in establishing a winning team. Gerry Phipps started attending team workouts and received the game ball after the Broncos upset Kansas City 33-27 in their first appearance under Speedie. During that game the "Go, Broncos, Go" chant was born at Bears Stadium. Speedie took time from the game to turn to the crowd and lead the cheers.

"We had lost our first four games," said Phipps, who became interim general manager when Faulkner was fired. "I could see something had to be done. I started going to practice, more as a learning experience than anything else. I felt I needed to know more about the operation before I could offer any help."

Even with a new coach and Gerry Phipps' new involvement the Broncos lost 11 games in 1964, including a 1-5-1 second-half record. In November Denver almost lost the Broncos. An irrevocable voting trust, controlling 52 per cent of Empire Sports, was formed by Cal Kunz, Ben Stapleton, James Stokes, Earl Howsam, Edward Hirschfeld and Walter Emery. The five-year-old Bronco operation was nearly $2 million in the red and the Kunz group wanted to sell the franchise.

Sam Lusky, *Sportscope* publisher, advertising executive, lifetime Bronco fan and adviser, clearly remembers how he first learned about the trust. "Allan invited me to have a drink with Gerry and Dick Kitchen," Lusky chuckled. "As I was raising my glass Gerry said, 'How does it feel to be drinking with the *minority* stockholders?' I almost dropped my drink. Then they explained the whole situation to me."

The "Voting Trust" became very unpopular in Denver. "The *Post* portrayed the Kunz group as the 'bad guys' and dressed the Phippses in white hats."

The "black hats" lined up three potential buyers—Chicago White Sox owner Arthur Allyn, Philadelphia toy manufacturer Nicholas Troilo and the Cox Broadcasting Company. Kunz reportedly received offers ranging from $3-5 million for Empire Sports. Cox' representatives were ready to buy the Broncos and move them to Atlanta, but they wanted *all* the stock and the Phippses adamantly refused to sell their share. Rather than operate with sizable minority stockholders looking over their shoulders, the Cox people left Denver empty handed.

Phipps then offered Kunz and company $1.5 million for their interests, vowing to keep the Broncos in Denver if the bid was accepted. It was, and he did. On February 15, 1965, Gerry and Allan Phipps owned Empire Sports.

"We are trying to attract industry to this community," Phipps later explained to *Sports Illustrated's* Edwin Shrake. "Nothing would hurt us more than headlines around the country saying Denver had lost its football team. I would be cutting my own throat if I did something that would set back the community, and if we can sell 20,000 season tickets we can break even financially."

AFL Commissioner Joe Foss visits with the Broncos' new owners — Gerry and Allan Phipps.

Phipps' signature on the contract signalled the start of an intense season-ticket drive. The entire Rocky Mountain region participated in the push to peddle ducats. *Denver Post* publisher Palmer Hoyt introduced a payroll-deduction plan permitting his employees to purchase tickets for 88 cents a week. The *Post* also carried "box scores" showing the drive's daily progress. More than 20 other companies adopted Hoyt's payroll-deduction plan.

Ron Hermes

Ron Hermes, a vice-president at People's Bank in Aurora, devised the "Bronco Note" concept, a no-interest, installed-payment loan scheme. Several other banks began offering the same service. By April 1, 1965, Phipps' goal of 20,000 tickets had been reached.

Encouraged by season-ticket sales, Gerry Phipps reorganized Empire Sports. He became Chairman of the Board and appointed his brother Allan president. Allan, an attorney, had been active in Bronco operations since 1962 when he purchased a piece of the Kunz-Howsam package. Veteran baseball administrator Jim Burris was named executive vice-president. Two prominent Denverites, Richard Kitchen and Robert Person, served on the board of directors. Kitchen, a nine-letter man at Loveland High School, a graduate of Yale University and Denver Law School and an ex-Marine company commander, and Person, president of the Public Service Company of Colorado, were later joined on the board by Burris. In a final administrative move Gerry Phipps hired Fred Gehrke as Bronco personnel director.

Gehrke followed Mac Speedie through high school and college in Utah, excelling in track and diving until he gained enough weight for pro football. As a pro, Gehrke played for Cleveland, Los Angeles, San Francisco and the Chicago Cardinals. In 1945 Fred was on the Cleveland team that beat Frank Filchock and the Redskins 15-14 for the NFL title.

Fred Gehrke

Gehrke was honored by the NFL Hall of Fame in 1972 for designing helmet insignias. "It was the first design ever associated with a team name—the Rams," reminisced Fred. "I sketched a black-and-white profile, then painted one and showed it to the owners. They went wild—told me to do them all. So I had about 75 helmets in my garage. I painted 5 or 6 a night—more on the weekends. We had to keep cans of paint in the locker room to retouch them when they got chipped."

Gehrke was pleased by Gerry Phipps' growing role in Bronco activities. "I have played and worked for several owners," stated Denver's current assistant general manager. "Gerry Phipps is the greatest of them all. He is in the background until you need him. Then he is always there."

Shortly after Gehrke's appointment the AFL expanded. Miami, the first new team, selected Ed Cooke, Tom Erlandson, Tom Nomina and John McGeever from Denver's "unprotected" list. A year later the Broncos lost Pat Matson, Cookie Gilchrist, Mike Kellogg, Henry Sorrell, Lonnie Wright and Andre White to Cincinnati, the second new AFL team.

The 1965 Broncos led the AFL West in attendance, receiving numerous sitting ovations during their dismal 4-10 season. The only bright spot was one of Denver's best defensive efforts ever. On October 3, 1965, the Broncos bombed the New York Jets 16-13, holding young Joe Namath and his explosive Easterners to just 205 total yards. Jet Jim Turner kicked 47 and 49-yard field goals, but Gary Kroner booted three three-pointers and Wendell Hayes scored from two yards out with less than a minute left to play. Almost 35,000 fans enjoyed the dual celebration — the Bronco win and co-owner Allan Phipps' 53rd birthday.

Once again the Broncos had a miserable second half, winning only one of their last seven games. Denver's sub-par performance did not deter attendance. With an average of more than 30,000 people per game, Bears Stadium was rapidly becoming inadequate. In March 1966 Governor John Love signed into law an act creating a four-county metropolitan district and subjecting a bond issue for financing a new stadium to public vote within one year.

Three months later the American and National Football Leagues merged. NFL Commissioner Pete Rozelle, who would preside over both new *conferences,* made the historic announcement.

Since pre-season inter-league play did not begin until 1967, Mac Speedie was not affected by the merger. As a head coach Speedie survived only two games in 1966, including the Broncos worst offensive outing in history. On September 3, opening day at Houston, Denver's Goldie Sellers returned a kickoff 88 yards for a touchdown. The Oilers won 45-7, allowing the Broncos no first downs during the entire game.

Speedie resigned on September 18, 1966. Former players thought Mac was, "knowledgeable, open and extremely fair." A Bronco official called Mac, "a victim of circumstances; a good coach blessed with a wealth of bad talent." Several receivers, including Lionel Taylor, credit Speedie with teaching them improved pass-catching techniques. Now a Bronco scout, the soft-spoken Speedie is highly respected by his pro football peers.

Ray Malavasi, an aide at Denver since 1962, was appointed interim coach. A player at West Point and Mississippi State and a coach at Mississippi State and Memphis State, Malavasi was described by ex-Broncos as, "the best defensive coach in football; an innovator; a square shooter; and a hard worker." Ray had no better luck than his three predecessors, winning just four of the 12 remaining games in 1966.

On December 19, 1966, Lou Saban signed a 10-year pact as Bronco head coach and general manager. Saban told newsmen, "Phipps offered me a contract that knocked my eyes out." The two-time AFL Coach of the Year was a single-wing quarterback at Indiana University before playing defense in the AFC. Saban and Speedie were teammates on Cleveland's four-time championship team. Lou retired in 1949, after the AFC's last season. Before becoming a Bronco he led Boston and Buffalo in the AFL and coached college ball at Washington, Case, Northwestern, Western Michigan and Maryland.

Denver rolled out the red carpet for Saban. He responded to the warm welcome by saying, "The challenge of directing the Denver Broncos, both on the field and off, is the most stimulating assignment I have undertaken during the years I have been associated with football." Little did Lou know Denver voters were about to slap local pro football square in the face.

On March 7, 1967, with or without knowing that passage would assure the permanency of the Bronco franchise, an unexpected 150,000 Denver property owners defeated the $20 million bond issue to finance a multi-purpose metropolitan stadium. Bond issue backers could not explain the overwhelming loss.

One supporter, Golden attorney Tom Carney, told the Post, "Frankly, I don't know what happened. All I can say is the people apparently don't want to subject their property to a mill levy for the new stadium."

Denver Mayor Tom Currigan commented, "The importance of professional sports to a community is so vital we simply cannot afford to give it up. Obviously a different plan for implementation and a more effective job of informing the public are now required."

"I am shocked and deeply disappointed," added Gerry Phipps. "We will have to evaluate the reason for the vote against it. If it was a lack of confidence in our organization—or the ownership—that's one thing. If it was a taxpayer's revolt, that's something else again.

Sam Lusky called it a "protest" vote. "I knew something was wrong when the fire houses started calling in. Our surveys and research showed the vote would be about three to one in favor. The early returns were about three to one against."

"The timing was bad," said Bob McCullough, Bronco turned stockbroker. "A few months before the stadium thing, Denver voters had just approved a multi-million dollar civic improvement issue."

Sports writer Pasquale Marranzino stated, "My own shallow analysis of the stadium defeat concerns vagueness and bad salesmanship on the part of the proponents."

New coach and GM Lou Saban concluded, "Whether we like it or not, it is going to make a tremendous negative impact on sports centers around the country. They are going to look at this result very carefully."

The final results, almost two to one against, surprised everyone. Lusky explained that the massive pro-stadium campaign made people respond to pre-vote surveys affirmatively rather than shame themselves by displaying a lack of civic pride. "They told our people they would vote for it," he said, "then they went out and turned the damn thing down."

Undaunted by the stadium defeat Saban began building an empire. He moved the organization to modern offices with adjacent practice fields and locker room facilities. He drafted and traded for many future Bronco stars and he helped develop Denver's up-to-date scouting system.

The Broncos beat Detroit 13-7 on August 5, 1967, becoming the first AFL team to defeat an NFL team. Saban was carried off the DU field after the historic victory. Denver closed out the pre-season with two more wins—a 14-9 upset over the Vikings and a 21-17 decision against Oakland. Before regulation play began Saban was questioned about the merger.

Denver's coach replied, "The merger saved pro football, saved some franchises. It is good for football. Of course, there is the old guard in the NFL that wanted to keep football the way it was. They do not want to cut up the pie. The AFL paid $25 million to merge, and that is an expensive handshake."

The Broncos opened the 1967 season by beating Boston 26-21, then won two of their next 13 games. Denver's poor showing did not stop the Dedicated Organization for the Erection of the Right kind of Stadium (DOERS) and similar groups from working on the bond issue problem. By February 1968 these groups had raised the nearly $2 million needed to pay off Bears Stadium's indebtedness. Gerry Phipps then deeded the stadium to Denver, allowing the city to finance the addition of 16,000 seats through self-repaying revenue bonds.

It was a financially complicated matter with a simple conclusion.

The Broncos were staying in Denver to play in a 50,000-plus seat stadium.

With injuries to key personnel— Steve Tensi, Al Denson and Floyd Little—the Broncos won five games in 1968. On October 13 Denver defeated the eventual World Champion New York Jets 21-13. On November 10 the Raiders beat the Broncos 43-7 before 50,002 fans—the first and last 50,000 crowd at "Bears" Stadium. In December a special committee selected "Mile High" from hundreds of new names submitted for the Bears-Broncos ballpark. Denver christened their newly named

stadium by losing to Kansas City 30-7.

In May 1969 Commissioner Rozelle announced the new NFL alignment. Denver was not happy with the arrangement. "We were the last stumbling block," said Gerry Phipps. "They put us in too tough a division. We thought continued losing would hurt attendance. We finally agreed when it was decided that Denver would be the only AFC team to host four NFC teams each year during the first five-year scheduling sequence. We felt having old, established NFL teams play in Denver would stimulate interest."

Since 1919 when George Calhoun and Curly Lambeau organized them, the Green Bay Packers were an old, established team. "The Pack" convinced fans that the NFL was a far superior league by badly beating AFL opponents in the first two Super Bowls. The third championship clash pried open a few closed minds.

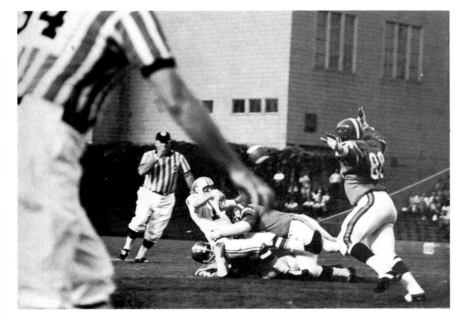

23

Prior to the January showdown Tex Maule wrote, "The pro football championship was rather definitely decided on a mushy field on December 29 when the Baltimore Colts crushed the Browns 34-0 for the NFL title, but the Colts will have to ratify that claim in Miami this Sunday when they play the New York Jets."

In another pre-Super Bowl III *SI* story Maule carefully listed and defended all the reasons the Jets could not possibly beat the Colts. "With the common draft of the last two years," he prophesied, "the AFL is getting its share of the truly competitive gung-ho athletes and it will soon achieve parity with the NFL. But that parity has not yet been reached, and the Colts should demonstrate this with an authority that may shock Jets fans."

Well . . . a brash young man from the University of Alabama repaid Sonny Werblin's $400,000 investment that Sunday. Broadway Joe Namath led his Jets and the AFL to a 16-7 super-upset. When Kansas City repeated by knocking off the powerful Vikings in Super Bowl IV, the AFL had achieved its parity.

A few months after Namath's miracle in Miami, ABC-TV announced *Monday Night Football* would begin in 1970. In his autobiography, *Cosell*, humble Howard explains how the program became, "in financial terms, the most successful sports package in history." He does not explain why the prime-time telecast avoided Mile High Stadium for three years.

Lou Saban plunged into 1969, the last non-*Monday Night Football* season, with high hopes. The Broncos posted a 5-8-1 record after opening the season with wins over Boston and the World Champion New York Jets. On October 19 Floyd Little rushed for 166 yards at Cincinnati, helping Denver beat the Bengals 30-23. On November 2, Denver posted their first shut-out ever, a 13-0 victory over San Diego. The Broncos also led the AFL with 45 quarterback sacks.

Joe Collier, all Big-Ten end at Northwestern University and a Saban aide in 1960 at Boston, 1962 at Buffalo and 1969 at Denver, thought the Bronco skill at "bump-and-run" set up those sacks. "If the receivers cannot get downfield," Collier commented, "the front four has more time to get to the quarterback. The bump-and-run all but vanished when the leagues merged, but the Broncos have continued their success at getting to the passer."

"The 1970 Broncos," said Lou Saban, "are headed in the right direction. The days of constant shuffling of personnel are over in Denver. We have a number of men who can take us where we want to go. We should be better both offensively and defensively. The only problem is that the other clubs will be better too. And there is no question that our division is the toughest in pro football . . ."

Floyd Little Day at Mile High Stadium — October 29, 1972.

"Offensively," the Bronco coach continued, "with Bob Anderson and Floyd Little in the backfield, we will have real explosiveness. The receiving, with Al Denson, Mike Haffner, John Embree and Bill Van Heusen, could rate with the best . . .

"Defensively, Rick Jackson and Dave Costa anchor a line we think is solid. Cornerback Bill Thompson is a standout in the secondary . . . Overall, we look for a better Denver Bronco football team in 1970."

The Broncos beat Buffalo, Pittsburgh and Kansas City; lost to Oakland; then defeated Atlanta in their first five games. Second-half horrors haunted our heroes again. In their last seven games the Broncos were 1-5-1. They finished the season with a 5-8-1 record and managed to lead the 26-team NFL with 63 punt returns.

"This is the year," said Saban about 1971. "We must start moving in the direction of a winning season. We were very close last year, but evidently we were not quite tough enough to maintain our fast start. This year we feel we have enough quality players, granting some are rookies, to make up some of the ground we need to become a winner."

Unable to make up any ground in the first nine games of the season, Saban suddenly resigned as Bronco head coach on November 17, 1971. He relinquished his GM post a month later. Saban's 20-42-3 record was a new longevity mark in Denver coaching history. Bronco brass, fans and players, who had cheered and booed Lou for five years, had mixed reactions about his departure.

Joe Collier

Gerry Phipps called it a tragedy. "When Lou came here in 1966," he said, "the organization was in pretty sad shape. We looked to Lou to bring us respectability in all phases of the operation. And he has done an absolutely superb job of it."

Others were not as appreciative of Saban's efforts. "He belittled his players," said one of the many Broncos swept out of Denver in a massive housecleaning. Another commented, "He was an authoritarian. He had a big-man image. The 'yes-sir' players loved him."

"He was dishonest, two-faced and too conservative," an ex-quarterback quipped. "Lou either liked you or did not like you. Once that was settled, he would not change his mind regardless of your performance."

Some of Saban's trades linked with his continuous rebuilding program angered fans. A 1973 *Sportscope* editorial warned, "It is just depressingly possible that the five unproductive Saban years in which we gave away more talent than we kept will come back to haunt us."

"Not true," argued Fred Gehrke. "Saban did more for Denver than any previous coach. You had to understand Lou. He fired me twice a day. Lou was an old-time coach—some guys could not play for him, others cried when he left. His biggest mistake was bringing in too many young college coaches. He ended up coaching his coaches instead of concentrating on other things. Lou was outwardly hard—he had to be. But once you got to know him, he was soft and decent inside."

Offensive line coach Jerry Smith filled the vacancy for the remainder of 1971. Smith, all Big-Ten at the University of Wisconsin, retired in 1956 after a pro career with the San Francisco 49ers and Green Bay Packers. Smith returned to football in 1959 as line coach at Dayton. He joined Saban's staff at Boston in 1960, shuffled off to Buffalo with Lou in 1962, and worked for the Cleveland Browns and New Orleans Saints before coming to Denver in 1971.

Smith's Broncos won two of their final five games, making their 1971 record 4-9-1. After the season Denver again needed a head coach and general manager. Gerry Phipps, in his own words, "too anxious to get the thing settled," tried to hire Bill Petersen. Petersen accepted the Bronco job without mentioning he had already signed a contract with the Houston Oilers. Phipps continued his search and eventually uncovered a treasure on the West Coast.

Stanford President Richard Lyman discussed Phipps' find. "John Ralston has done a magnificent job here," said Lyman, " and we are going to miss him. He has understood the importance of treating student-athletes as mature and thoughtful people. We intend to maintain that tradition at Stanford. I know thousands of Stanford people join me in wishing John and Patty every good fortune as they take up an exciting new life in Denver."

Ralston started his "exciting new life in Denver" with a whirlwind round of speaking engagements. His tour included a stop at the University of Colorado Denver Center to lecture a sports psychology class. He opened his speech by displaying the cover picture of his book, *Coaching Today's Athlete,* showing an impossible block a Stanford end had made. "Sheer desire and dedication," the newest Bronco boss said.

A student in the class asked Ralston about the instability and insecurity of a coaching career in any sport. Confident John replied, "Only losing coaches need worry about their jobs."

Ralston's confidence is becoming legendary. "He predicted a 10-4 season," *Sports Illustrated's* Joe Marshall wrote in 1972. "When the team's record reached 1-4 he was asked what his new prediction was. Ralston reacted as if it were a trick question. Why wouldn't it still be 10-4? Skeptics tapped their temples and exchanged meaningful glances. That weekend the Broncos beat Oakland for the first time in 10 years."

In only three seasons have Ralston's teams dropped below .500—in 1959, his first year at Utah State; in 1963, his first year at Stanford; and in 1972, his first year at Denver. Apparently it takes John a year to get his message across.

"Well, sure," Ralston said. "But my basic philosophy is if you hang in there tough enough, long enough, work hard enough, dedicate yourself with a positive approach, anything can be accomplished."

"The positive approach" has become Ralston's trademark. It goes way back according to Mrs. Ralston. Patty's contribution to *Coaching Today's Athlete* provides readers with a great insight to her husband as a player, a coach and a person. She states John's desire to coach a Rose Bowl team started when he played linebacker in the classic twice for Lynn Waldorf's University of California teams.

Patty Ralston also writes about having the Utah and Stanford squads into their home the night before games to relax the players and establish a feeling of team unity. She concludes her chapter by stressing the importance of a coach's wife. "There are few professions other than coaching," she claims, "where a wife can be a bigger help or hindrance. Your peace of mind and empathy in most instances will give him needed strength and understanding in a profession that consists of a myriad of factors, all of which evolve around emotion."

Ralston includes an in-depth self-analysis in *Coaching Today's Athlete*. In the introduction he lists, "five precepts by which we attempt to pattern our personal lives; they have become important components of our profession which we diligently attempt to impart to our players:

1. A burning desire to win or to be successful;

2. The creation of a compulsion to improve at all times, either through direction or self-improvement;

3. To possess a singular virtue of stick-to-itiveness;

4. To be honest, possess integrity, humility, and to observe spiritual values;

5. To be flexible in meeting the desires, needs and individual requirements for fulfillment."

A statement later in the book explains Ralston's extraordinary rapport with his players. "Today's coach is confronted with young people who wish to try various styles of life, to test traditional beliefs and values, and they often rebel against the 'establishment' while advocating what they believe to be new or inventive. Now, more than ever, we coaches must re-evaluate ourselves and our programs. We must take another look at our goals, our general and specific philosophies, our ethics and our relationships with our players."

Ralston's first official Bronco business was to organize a new war council. He retained Joe Collier as defensive coordinator. Max Coley left the Steelers to become Denver's offensive coordinator. Ralston hired his Stanford assistant Bob Gambold to coach the linebackers. "Doc" Urich quit coaching the Buffalo Bills defensive line to perform the same job for the Broncos. Oregon head coach Jerry Frei took over the offensive line. Dick Coury, former California State-Fullerton head coach, came to Denver to handle the wide receivers. And Myrel Moore left California at Berkeley to coach the Broncos special teams. Ralston's new crew compiled a 5-9 record in 1972 before posting two straight winning seasons in 1973 and 1974.

"No team was more ripe for Ralston than the Denver Broncos," said Bob McCullough. "John attacked the players' minds. He taught the Broncos how to win."

"After Washington beat us 41-0 in pre-season," Sam Lusky added, "Ralston started his post-game speech by saying, 'Fellas, I saw a lot I like out there today.' He emphasizes the good and plays down the bad."

Ralston's positive approach is not confined to his players. He has also convinced himself. Readying for a racquet-ball match at Bronco headquarters, John admitted, "Since I've been coaching, I've wanted to coach in the College All-Star game. Through the years, they've switched it back and forth between college and pro coaches. Now the only way I can get there is by winning the Super Bowl—but that's fine with me."

"John Ralston," said Gerry Phipps, "Has tremendous ambition to succeed in his profession. He thrives on challenges."

Only one more challenge stands between John Ralston and a trip to Chicago for the All-Star game some summer. He has discussed it several times: "It is an all-encompassing obsession of mine and my family's to go to and win the Super Bowl. Just like it was an all-encompassing obsession to go to and win the Rose Bowl. And it will happen sooner or later. It is inevitable."

Every day, as the Broncos trot from their training room to the practice field, they see the sign:

"Through These Doors Pass The Most Spirited Footballers In The NFL—The Mighty Broncos"

QUARTERBACKS

At both ends of Denver's football rainbow is not a pot of gold, but a quality quarterback. Between Frank Tripucka and Charley Johnson lie 13 losing seasons and a mind-boggling succession of signal callers. The Broncos auditioned more than 50 hopefuls and cast 22 different men in the starting role. Of these 22 starters, the first and last, Tripucka and Johnson, two shopworn old veterans, became the most popular and proficient passers in the long history of Bronco quarterbacks...

Denver's philosophy concerning quarterbacks has changed repeatedly since the birth of the Broncos. This instability is due to injuries, high turnover of coaches and owners, lack of depth at other positions, and fan pressure. Promising young quarterbacks lost their best years to injuries. New coaches made wholesale personnel changes which sapped the team's strength, especially on defense. And the fans, faithful through so many unsuccessful seasons have been extremely critical of quarterbacks.

Fan disapproval was often justified. Too many times, when someone was needed to step in and lead the offense, nobody was there. This void is hard to explain since 57 *qualified quarterbacks* have passed through the Bronco organization. Twenty-two appeared in regular season games. If Charley Johnson can play until 1980 Denver will have averaged one active quarterback per year.

John Hufnagel—*Denver's hope for the future*

The fans, however, were occasionally wrong. Their criticism went too far and they did not know all the facts. The Bronco booster is quick to blame one man when many are at fault. A few bad passes prompt pleas for a different quarterback. One recently departed QB commented, "Denver fans sure like new faces."

Bronco management recruited numerous new faces for their loyal throng. An army of collegiate stars and men who succeeded on other pro teams were unable to solve the Broncos' quarterback problems. They came to Denver with impressive credentials.

Name	Position	Height	Weight	College	Year With Broncos
BAKER, Jimmy	QB	6-2	195	East Tennessee	64
BEARD, Mickey	QB	6-0	180	Dartmouth	68
BEBAN, Gary	QB	6-1	195	UCLA	71
BIGGS, Bob	QB	5-11	180	Cal-Davis	74
BLACKFORD, Craig	QB	6-3	220	Evansville	71
BREAUX, Don	QB	6-1	205	McNeese St.	63
BRISCOE, Marlin	QB	5-10	177	Omaha	68
CALCAGNO, Ray	QB	6-0	185	Santa Clara	68
CHOBOIAN, Max	QB	6-4	205	San Fernando St.	66
CONNER, Mike	QB	6-4	212	North Dakota	71
CORCORAN, Jim	QB	6-0	200	Maryland	67
DiVITO, Joe	QB	6-2	190	Boston College	68
DUBLINSKI, Tom	QB	6-2	205	Utah	60
EGLOFF, Rick	QB	6-2	190	Wyoming	68
ENIS, Hunter	QB	6-2	195	TCU	62
ERNST, Mike	QB	6-1	190	Cal-Fullerton	72
GLACKEN, Scotty	QB	6-0	190	Duke	66-7
GORMAN, Ed	QB	6-4	215	Portland St.	69
GREEN, Charlie	QB	6-1	200	Wittenberg	69
HERRING, George	QB	6-2	200	Southern Miss.	60-1
HORN, Don	QB	6-2	195	San Diego St.	71-2
HERTZFELD, Gary	QB	6-1	190	Utah	65
HUFNAGEL, John	QB	6-1	195	Penn State	73-4
HYSON, Dick	QB	6-1	200	Colorado	60
JOHNSON, Charley	QB	6-1	200	New Mexico St.	72-4
KENT, Mailon	QB	6-2	193	Auburn	67
KISSINGER, Elis	QB	5-11	185	Southern Cal.	60
LECLAIR, Jim	QB	6-1	208	C. W. Post	67-8
LEE, Jacky	QB	6-1	187	Cincinnati	64-5
LISKE, Pete	QB	6-2	195	Penn State	69-70
LUCAS, Richie	QB	6-2	190	Penn State	62
MAY, Roger	QB	6-1	185	Vanderbilt	68
McCALL, Bernie	QB	6-2	195	Colorado	68
McCORMICK, John	QB	6-1	210	Massachusetts	63, 5, 6, 8
McCUNE, Allen	QB	6-2	195	West Virginia	66
MILLER, Ron	QB	6-0	190	Wisconsin	63
MOBLEY, Carlos	QB	6-1	190	Auburn	62
MONROE, Jim	QB	5-11	185	Arkansas	60
O'BRIEN, Buster	QB	6-1	195	Richmond	69
PASTRANA, Al	QB	6-1	193	Maryland	69-70
PHIPPS, Joe	QB	5-11	185	Northern Michigan	63
RAMSEY, Steve	QB	6-2	210	North Texas St.	71-4
REED, Mark	QB	6-0	185	Arizona	68
ROTE, Tobin	QB	6-3	220	Rice	66
SHAW, George	QB	6-0	185	Oregon	62
SKELTON, Bobby	QB	5-11	180	Alabama	61
SLAUGHTER, Mickey	QB	6-0	190	Louisiana Tech	63-6
STAVROFF, Frank	QB	6-1	200	Indiana	67
STEWART, Bob	QB	6-2	205	Northern Arizona	70
STOFA, John	QB	6-3	210	Buffalo	72
SURINA, Jack	QB	5-11	180	Cal Poly-Pomona	74
TENSI, Steve	QB	6-5	220	Florida State	67-70
TRIPUCKA, Frank	QB	6-2	208	Notre Dame	60-3
WEIDNER, Gale	QB	6-1	195	Colorado	62
WILKIE, Dennis	QB	6-0	180	Toledo	61
WILSON, George Jr.	QB	6-1	180	Xavier	68
WOOD, Dick	QB	6-5	200	Auburn	62

Craig Blackford was three-time all-conference at Indiana University. Hunter Enis, acquired from San Diego, led TCU to the 1948 conference championship. John Stofa set an AFL record for interception avoidance with the Bengals in 1968.

Bob Stewart passed for 2,123 yards and 18 touchdowns his senior year at Northern Arizona University. Gary Beban won the 1967 Heisman trophy at UCLA. Bernie McCall compiled 3,059 yards total offense in three years at the University of Colorado.

Rick Egloff, acquired from Oakland, led the Wyoming Cowboys to a 10-1 record, including a victory over Florida State in the Sun Bowl. Roger May led the Southeastern Conference in interception avoidance and completed 55 percent of his passes for 929 yards and nine touchdowns during his senior year at Vanderbilt. Jim Corcoran set passing records at the University of Maryland.

George Shaw gained football fame as "the man Johnny Unitas replaced" after Shaw suffered a severe broken leg at Baltimore. Shaw's 97-yard TD pass to Jerry Tarr in 1962 is still a Bronco record.

Mike Ernst set season and career records at Cerritos Junior College and won Small College All-American honors at Cal State-Fullerton. Allen McCune passed for five touchdowns and ran for a sixth to give West Virginia a 63-48 win over Pittsburgh.

Joe DiVito holds the Bronco record for shortest career. DiVito, from Boston College, played in two games—one for 10 seconds and the other for less than two minutes. Tobin Rote, Denver's oldest quarterback at 38, was once outstanding in the AFL and NFL.

Mike Ernst

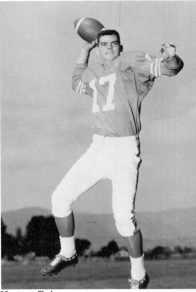

Hunter Enis

These quarterbacks and others were tested and eventually failed to deliver for Denver. They saw little or no action. With the exception of "King" Corcoran, a current WFL QB, the Broncos have never released a quarterback who went on to stardom elsewhere. Few achieved stardom here although many had their chances.

The Broncos have had some super second-string signal callers starting with George Herring. Herring was the nation's fifth leading college punter and led Mississippi Southern to number one small-college honors in 1956. George started and completed only one Bronco game. His six interceptions in that game set a team record. "I'll never forget it," he said. "I threw the ball 40 times and players made catches all over the field. It didn't matter what color jerseys they were wearing."

Herring had a short, tough career with Denver. He usually watched while Frank Tripucka ran the offense. Not knowing when or if he would play, George seldom had a chance to warm up before going into action. Herring quit prior to the 1962 season.

George Shaw

George Herring

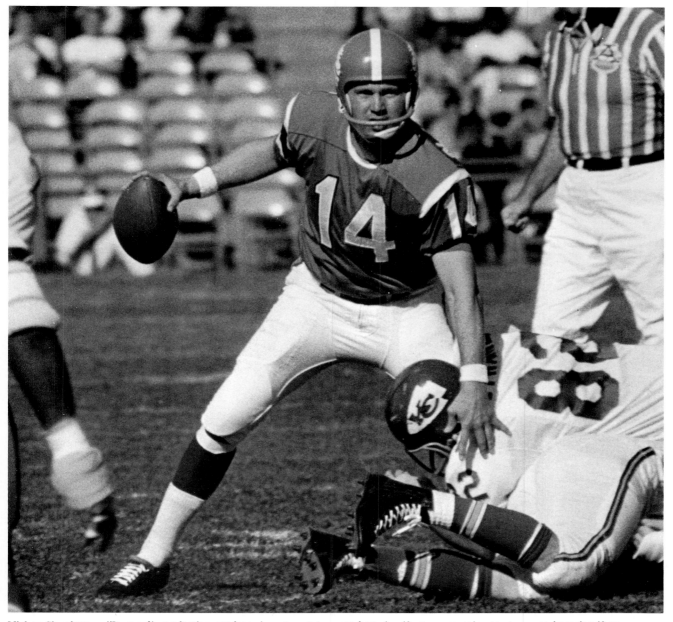

Mickey Slaughter — "It was discomforting not knowing your status—not knowing if you were going to start—not knowing if an interception or bad call would get you pulled out. The coaches were looking for a 'take charge guy' and nobody was doing the job."

Herring's retirement made room for Dick "Stork Legs" Wood. Wood, an ex-War Eagle, played for five AFL teams—San Diego, Denver, New York, Oakland and Miami—in five years. Wood had weak legs and a strong arm. His passes could knock receivers down. Dick was activated on December 6, 1962, in time for the last two games. He played in neither.

While Wood wandered through the AFL, the Broncos drafted Mickey Slaughter in 1963. Mickey completed 58.5 percent of his passes at Louisiana Tech and made the Dean's list four times. When Frank Tripucka retired, Slaughter became Denver's starting quarterback. Mickey's career was plagued by job insecurity, injuries and Bronco fans.

1905175

35

Mickey's injuries include four concussions during his college and pro career. He hurt one shoulder in 1965 then dislocated the other a few games later. The following year, at age 25, Mickey retired.

"Slaughter," John McCormick bitterly remembers, "had just three games to go to get his pension. His injuries were a part of it, but the fans were so rough on Mickey, he just didn't want to put his uniform on again. So he quit."

Slaughter had a mixed record at Denver. His 34 completions is still a Bronco single-game record. He is among the leaders in all career passing categories. Slaughter appeared in 32 games, started 19, completed three, and took part in only four victories. He was also involved in four of Denver's most memorable defeats—59-7 to Kansas City in 1963; 40-7 to Oakland in 1964; 45-10 to New York in 1965; and the "no-first-down" game, a 45-7 loss to Houston in 1966. Against the Oilers that day, Denver quarterbacks (Slaughter and John McCormick) completed two of 20 passes for a one-yard loss. Three weeks after the humiliation at Houston, Mickey retired.

The job insecurity was vividly illustrated on October 4, 1964. Slaughter and Jacky Lee played in Denver's "musical quarterback" game against Boston. Lee started, threw an interception in the first quarter, and was replaced by Slaughter. Lee returned in the middle of the second quarter, but Mickey finished the first half. Lee started the third quarter and yielded to Slaughter with six minutes left. Jacky played the first few series of the fourth quarter. After the seventh quarterback change, Slaughter finished the game.

Slaughter's departure left limping John McCormick in charge of Denver's offense. McCormick, All-Yankee Conference at Massachusetts, originally signed with Minnesota in 1962. John was the Viking punter as a rookie and he played QB behind Fran Tarkenton. In 1963, three days after receiving the game ball for his performance in the last exhibition game, John was released.

"I talked to San Francisco on the phone," McCormick recalls, "and agreed to go out there. Then Jack Faulkner called and asked me to stop in Denver on my way out. Jack met me at the airport. I only had a two-hour layover, but he had borrowed a brand new convertible for me to use and reserved a big suite at the Hilton. I saw Cal Kunz. He bettered the 49er offer, so I signed with Denver. Right after I signed Jack said he had to return the car. Then he convinced me it would be more practical—closer to the practice field—for me to stay at the Continental Denver."

McCormick's career started and ended quicker than anyone could have predicted.

John McCormick — "You cannot play when you know as soon as you make a mistake, you are going to sit down. You lose the 'momentum factor'—never knowing which quarterback will play."

The Broncos began 1963 with veteran Frank Tripucka, rookie Mickey Slaughter and Big Mac. After two games—five interceptions in 15 attempts—Tripucka quit football. Slaughter started the third game, but was injured in the third quarter. With Boston leading 10-0, McCormick came in and engineered a 14-10 Denver victory. The following week John passed for 265 yards and three touchdowns in a 50-34 romp over the Chargers. It looked like the Broncos had found a replacement for Slaughter and Tripucka—until McCormick's next game.

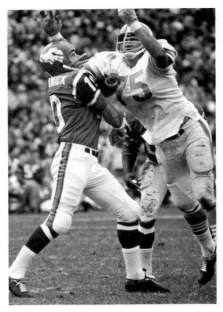

In the second quarter against Houston, John was sacked in Denver's end zone. He hurt his knee badly. Despite a gallant effort to continue his career, McCormick never fully recovered from that injury. Mac played briefly in two late 1963 games and underwent surgery in the off-season. The operation was unsuccessful. John spent the 1964 season in the pressbox.

He had a second operation in February, 1965, while the Phipps brothers were buying the Broncos. John played 10 games in 1965 and 10 more in 1966, but he never regained his pre-injury form.

"I couldn't move as well," John admits. "And to be quite honest, I was a little gun-shy. My confidence was gone and playing hurt took the fun out of football. The fans became unbearable. I had to change my home phone number four times."

The wounded knee and unsympathetic fans pushed McCormick out of football after the last 1966 game. He tried to return in 1968. In the season opener against Cincinnati he completed eight of 19 passes for 89 yards. Denver lost 24-10. When John left the field, he left for good.

cky Lee

Looking back, the historic "lend-lease" trade involving Jacky Lee was a bad deal. The Broncos, suffering from "win now" fever, gave Houston aging Bud McFadin, a second-round draft choice (which the Oilers wasted on NFL-bound Charley Taylor), and cash for the *two year use* of Lee.

Lee impressed Bronco brass in his first pro start. In 1960 the University of Cincinnati rookie threw touchdown passes of 78, 92, and 73 yards to defeat Denver 20-10. Lee spent most of the next four seasons on the bench behind George Blanda. During that period Jacky completed 170 passes for 2,995 yards and 23 touchdowns. He also set two AFL records—throwing for 457 yards against Boston and completing a 98-yard TD pass against San Diego.

Lee looked forward to temporary duty in Denver. He was eager to prove himself a capable starter. In 1964 he started 10 Bronco games and relieved Slaughter in the other four. In 1965 the Broncos realized Lee would be returning to Houston and used him sparingly in only three games.

McCormick and Slaughter were two-fifths of the 1963-66 quarterback shuffle. Players went in and out of games so often it was difficult to keep track of their names or assess their abilities. The other members of Denver's "five-man plan" were Jacky Lee, Don Breaux and Max Choboian.

McNeese State star Don Breaux joined Lee, Slaughter and McCormick in "quarterback roulette." Don was another of Denver's good backup quarterbacks. He had two starts and seven Bronco appearances. Of these games, Denver lost six and tied one. Breaux completed almost 51 percent of his passes and still holds the team record for interception avoidance.

Max Choboian, from San Fernando State, completed the quarterback quintet of 1963-66. Max supposedly came to camp as a personal favor to another coach. He was the only quarterback Denver sent to the "minors." The Broncos suggested that Max spend a year in the Continental League. Choboian worked hard at Norfolk, studying game films, trying to strengthen his arm and attempting to overcome his natural awkwardness.

Choboian started the 1966 season behind Slaughter and McCormick on the QB depth chart. With Mickey and John injured, Max started the seventh game. Kansas City beat the Broncos 56-10. Two weeks later Choboian posted his first pro win. His last-minute 65-yard touchdown pass to Al Denson defeated Boston 17-10. Of seven Choboian starts in 1966, Denver won three games. In 1967 Max lost his job to a trio of Bronco newcomers—Scotty Glacken, Jim Leclair and Steve Tensi.

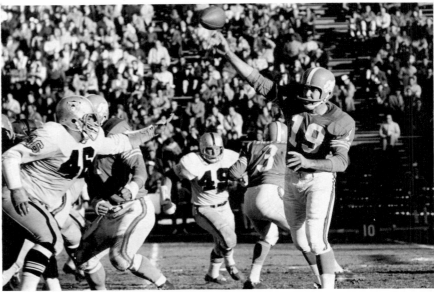

Don Breaux

Max Choboian

Scotty Glacken set Duke University career passing records with 255 completions in 480 attempts for 3,170 yards and 24 touchdowns. He joined the Broncos in 1966 and played briefly in three games. In 1967 Glacken led Denver to the 13-7 pre-season victory over Detroit. The Broncos were the first AFL team to ever defeat an NFL team.

"Glacken is mechanically a good thrower," said offensive coach Hunter Enis. "He can throw the short and long pass, the soft one or the bullet. Scott must learn timing. We expect him to hit the receiver at the right time. The receiver is running through traffic and will be open for only a second or so, just an eyeblink. You've got to hit him quick."

"On long passes," the ex-quarterback continued, "things are different. He must be right on the button if the receiver is there, or lob it over the defender's head to eliminate an interception. Learning timing is the difference between a passer and a thrower."

Glacken's pre-season fame did not carry over into the regular season. Scotty was zero for four in the second 1967 game. He never played again.

Glacken rode the bench with Jim Leclair, a San Francisco draft choice in 1966. To earn a spot on the 49ers, all Jim had to do was beat out John Brodie, Bill Kilmer or George Mira. Unable to do so, Jim spent his first pro season on the taxi squad, getting an education from 49er QB coach Y. A. Tittle.

Scotty Glacken — "Against Detroit, Coach Saban let me call all but two or three plays. He showed a lot of confidence in me. I called about 30 percent audibles—it should have been more. In college I usually changed plays 50 or 60 percent of the time."

Jim Leclair — "I got in for one play against Miami. I called a pass, naturally, and they blitzed two guys up the middle. I remember seeing Wahoo McDaniel right before I got slightly killed."

Leclair looked forward to making the team in 1967, but the 49ers drafted Steve Spurrier. "Spurrier's no-cut contract," a sportswriter observed, "makes Leclair's future a no-future." San Francisco put the C. W. Post star on waivers in August. Jack White, the 49ers general manager, had second thoughts about losing Leclair. White reportedly told Jim to stay out of sight until the waivers expired.

Word reached Leclair that Denver was looking for someone to replace John McCormick and Mickey Slaughter. "I heard the Broncos were interested in me," Jim said. "They had drafted Tom Cassesse from C. W. Post and saw me throwing to him in some films. So, when White told me to disappear, I drove to Denver."

The Broncos gave Leclair a playbook and hid him in training camp. Jim was in uniform, ready to report to practice, when the 49ers cancelled the waivers. Jim went back to San Francisco, only to be put on waivers again. This time he cleared and signed with Denver. Jim was activated and played against the Dolphins in the third 1967 game.

He started the sixth game against Buffalo. Jim was rolling along, enjoying a 16-3 lead, when disaster struck. A costly fumble, an unsuccessful fake punt and five missed field goals turned an apparent Bronco win into a 17-16 loss. It was the closest Leclair ever came to victory. In his second start Kansas City won 52-9. The next week Leclair and Steve Tensi were sacked 11 times by Oakland in a 21-17 loss. Leclair played seven games during his two-year Bronco career. Denver lost all of them.

Steve Tensi

In 1968 the Broncos could have fielded an entire offensive team of quarterbacks. The depth chart listed 11 names—John McCormick, Steve Tensi, Jim Leclair, Mickey Beard, Joe DiVito, Marlin Briscoe, Ray Calcagno, Rick Egloff, Mark Reed, Roger May and Bernie McCall. It looked like another year of "quarterback keno" until Steve Tensi shrugged his way into the starting spot.

Tensi joined the Broncos in 1967. San Diego received Denver's first draft choice in both 1968 and 1969 for Steve. It was an expensive trade, especially since the Broncos passed over Tensi *three times* in the 1965 draft. "As dear as the price was," Lou Saban explained, "we needed help immediately at quarterback. I believe Steve can step right in and help us."

Steve stepped in against Minnesota in pre-season, 1967. He arrived in Denver a few days before the game and was not expected to play. Hunter Enis gave Tensi wrist bands with plays written on them. Telling Enis "I don't need them," Steve tore the bands off, went into the game and passed the Broncos to a 14-9 victory. It was Denver's second straight win over an NFL team.

During 1967 Steve alternated with Jim Leclair. Tensi threw two touchdowns on opening day to beat Boston 26-21. The Broncos lost their next nine games. Tensi absorbed much of the blame for these losses, but Denver's mediocre offensive line and weak defense were more accurately at fault. The Broncos allowed more points than any other AFL team. Steve actually had a good year. He threw 16 touchdowns and gave up 17 interceptions—an excellent ratio. Those interceptions and Steve's awkward size made him the butt of many unkind jokes.

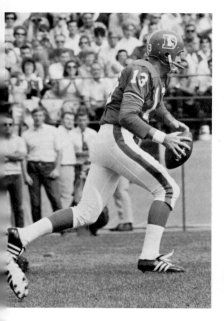

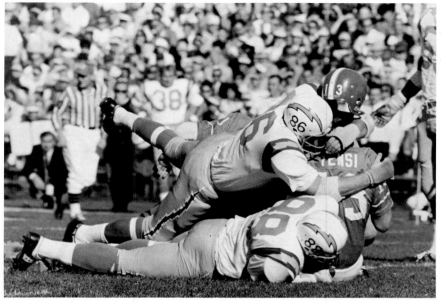

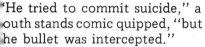

"He tried to commit suicide," a south stands comic quipped, "but the bullet was intercepted."

"Tensi fell in sections," another man observed.

A common comment was, "Tensi is the dumbest quarterback ever to play the game." Steve's appearance and crude manner were misinterpreted as a lack of intelligence.

Criticism of Tensi did not include his arm—probably the strongest in Denver quarterback history. Quarterbacks warm up in practice by facing each other a few yards apart. As they throw the ball back and forth,

they increase the distance between them. Toward the end of these drills all the passers are straining to reach one another. Steve stood easy, whipping long, graceful spirals without much apparent effort.

In 1968 Tensi broke his collarbone twice and played in only seven games. Denver won four of them. In 1969 and 1970 Steve had good passing years, but the interception myth was perpetuated. Whenever an opponent picked off a Tensi toss, Steve left the field in a thunderstorm of boos. Claims that Tensi threw too many interceptions and too few

touchdowns do not agree with the facts. Of Denver's 10 most prolific passers (more than 200 attempts), Tensi ranks second in interception avoidance and third in TD passes. In 39 games Steve threw 38 touchdowns. He was intercepted only 45 times in 810 attempts. Sacking the quarterback is a popular football phrase and an important defensive statistic. In Steve Tensi's case, credit Denver fans with one QB sack.

Give another sack to Bronco coaches who considered Marlin Briscoe too small. Briscoe's size did not bother him at the University of Omaha. He set 22 season and career records and averaged 201.6 yards total offense per game for four years. Marlin threw 52 touchdown passes, 25 in his senior year. As a pro, Briscoe was the primary quarterback in only seven Bronco games. He completed 102 passes and compiled a remarkable 17-yard gain per completion average.

Briscoe's blazing speed and catlike quickness brought Bronco fans several exciting afternoons. Marlin's major weakness was preferring to scramble rather than look for secondary receivers or dump the ball. "The Magician" could move the team and he put points on the scoreboard. Briscoe and Charley Johnson are the only two Denver quarterbacks who have thrown more touchdowns than interceptions.

Joe Collier claims, "The triple-threat quarterback gives me the most trouble. A man with a strong arm, one who uses the run well, and can get himself out of trouble drives defenses crazy. He can beat you so many ways."

Briscoe might have become a "triple-threat" quarterback. At contract time in 1969, Marlin demanded an impossible salary increase and insisted on being

signed exclusively at quarterback. Since the Broncos wanted to keep Briscoe, they pledged to use him *primarily* at quarterback. Marlin agreed and accepted the possibility of playing other positions. That left only a wide gap between the Broncos' bankroll and how much Marlin wanted. Reportedly the second-year pro was asking for a veteran quarterback's salary.

Unable to settle money matters and unable to trade Briscoe, the Broncos released him. Marlin eventually signed with Buffalo. In 1970 with the Bills, he led the AFC in receiving.

At San Diego in 1968—Marlin Briscoe receives last-second instructions from Hunter Enis. "The Magician" replaced Steve Tensi and threw three touchdowns in a 55-24 loss.

Pete Liske

With Briscoe gone the Broncos adopted a three quarterback system in 1969 and 1970. Stev Tensi alternated with Al Pastrana and Pete Liske.

Liske led Penn State to two Gator Bowls, then was drafted by the Jets in 1964. Pete playe briefly for New York before being traded to Buffalo in 196 There he watched Jack Kemp and Daryle Lamonica share the quarterbacking. Lou Saban, the Bills' coach, recommended tha Liske try Canadian football.

The CFL style of play meshed perfectly with Pete's abilities. I 1967 he led Calgary to the Western Conference champion-ship. His 303 completions and 4(touchdowns earned him league MVP honors. In 1968 Liske and the Stampeders won their first Grey Cup in 19 years. In four years Pete completed 843 passes for 12,836 yards and 95 touch-downs. Seeking a shot in the NF: he played out his option with Calgary and came south.

Bronco bosses just smiled and said "no comment" when askec about the "mystery quarter-back" visiting Denver in the summer of 1969. Rumor mills churned out stories about some "hot-shot" QB who purchased house and would soon be signir a contract. The mystery man w

Pete Liske, who could have been a Bronco six years earlier. He was the Jets' 15th draft choice.

So, instead of sharing the signal-calling chores with John McCormick, Mickey Slaughter and the 1963-66 QB crew, Liske split his game time with Tensi and Al Pastrana.

Steve started the 1969 season by throwing three touchdowns to beat Boston 26-21. He was injured in the second game against New York. Liske came in, passed for two TDs and a 21-19 win over the eventual world champions. Pete received the game ball for his first Bronco appearance.

Liske started and played the entire third game, a 41-28 loss to Buffalo. Pete passed 45 times for 289 yards and three touchdowns. He also suffered five interceptions and was sacked seven times. After that he was used only in relief of Tensi—until the last game of the season. He threw three touchdown passes to beat the Bengals 26-16.

The Broncos won four of their first five 1970 games with no real number-one quarterback. Liske started the first two, against Buffalo and Pittsburgh, but Tensi came in with Denver trailing and won both games. Of the remaining 12 games, Liske started seven, Pastrana three and Tensi two.

Fred Gehrke explained Liske's lack of success in the NFL. "His type of play and execution," Gehrke said, "were just right for Canadian football. But Liske didn't do so well here." The Broncos benched Pete late in 1970 to give Al Pastrana a three-game chance.

In his first start Pastrana completed five passes to Kansas City and was sacked six times as the Chiefs shutout Denver 16-0. Liske salvaged a 17-17 tie with San Diego in Pastrana's second outing. Al threw three more interceptions to end his Bronco career in a 27-13 loss to Cleveland.

Pastrana, "the kind of guy you would like for a son," set Atlantic Coast Conference passing records on Lou Saban's University of Maryland team. Lou brought Al to Denver, hoping to convert his college quarterback into pro material. In the "Great QB Purge" after the 1970 season, Pastrana, Liske and Tensi were replaced by two more new faces.

Al Pastrana

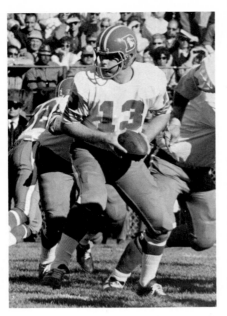

Saban traded Alden Roche and switched Denver's first-round draft position with Green Bay to obtain Don Horn. Most Bronco fans liked the trade. They felt a starting quarterback was more valuable than a promising, but unproven, defensive end.

Horn, heir apparent to Bart Starr, saw little action with Green Bay in 1967-68. In 1969 Don played in all 14 games. He set a Packer single-game record with 22 completions in 31 attempts for 410 yards and five touchdowns. In 1970 Don appeared in only seven games. He was traded to Denver the following year.

Broncoland went wild when Horn arrived. A man with a strong arm and four years experience behind Bart Starr was the answer to a prayer. With a little luck, 1971 would be *the year*. Unfortunately, that is exactly what Don Horn had at Denver—little luck.

Don defied superstition and chose to wear #13, his old Packer number. For Tensi tormentors, it was instant deja vu. On opening day the Broncos hosted Super Bowl-bound Miami in the famous "half-a-loaf" game. Saban settled for a 10-10 tie rather than risking a loss by going for a victory. Horn was

helplessly involved in a controversy concerning Saban's strategy. Two years later John Ralston made an identical, but much less criticized decision at St. Louis.

Horn's next start was against his old teammates in Milwaukee. Don threw no touchdowns and six interceptions (tying Herring's record) in a 34-13 loss. The following week he threw four more interceptions, dropping a 16-3 decision to Kansas City. Ten interceptions and no touchdowns in two straight weeks is a confidence-shattering experience for any quarterback. Some say Horn never recovered.

An injury and resignation drastically altered local pro football. On November 14, 1971, in the second quarter against Cincinnati, Don Horn separated his shoulder. He was never to play for the Broncos again. Horn, who came to Denver with plenty of publicity and the roar of marching bands, left town in an eerie silence. Another case of unfilled expectations and promise.

Three days after Horn's injury Lou Saban resigned. The last five games were left to assistant coach Jerry Smith and backup quarterback Steve Ramsey.

Don Horn

Steve Ramsey

John Hufnagel

The substitute pair won twice. Ramsey, two-time All-Missouri Valley at North Texas State, set NCAA records with 491 completions for 7,076 yards and 69 *touchdowns*. He was drafted by New Orleans in 1970, spent his rookie year on the Saints' taxi squad, and was traded to Denver in 1971.

Ramsey started 1972 as Denver's number one quarterback. Steve opened the season with 261 yards passing and a 30-17 victory over Houston. The Broncos lost their next four games. In game six, against Oakland, new coach John Ralston started old quarterback Charley Johnson. Charley completed 20 of 28 passes for 361 yards, two touchdowns and a 30-23 upset. Steve Ramsey has been Johnson's backup man since.

The third man in Denver's current quarterback corps is John Hufnagel. Hufnagel was Denver's 14th draft choice in 1973. John set nine passing records at Penn State. He threw for 2,201 yards and 20 touchdowns during his senior year. So far, with the exception of the all-rookie 1974 pre-season, John has seen only spot action with the Broncos.

Frank Tripucka — "We always had the talent, but we never had the organization. We used to make up plays in the huddle—'okay, who wants to go out for a pass?' On blocking assignments I was up at the line of scrimmage pointing to guys on the other team. When they put two guys over the center I knew I was doomed to wind up on my behind because all we ever blocked was the man on our nose."

Charley Johnson's Oakland start ended a decade of indecision that began in 1963 when Frank Tripucka retired. Frank's career started in 1946 on Frank Leahy's Notre Dame team. In 1948 "Tripper" led the Irish to an undefeated season.

As a pro in the National, Canadian and American Football Leagues, Tripucka completed 1,714 passes in 3,141 attempts for 22,732 yards. He still holds 10 major Bronco records: career—total offense, completions and touchdowns; season—total offense, completions and touchdowns; game—attempts, yards gained and touchdowns; and nine consecutive games with touchdown passes.

"I knew Frank at the end of his career," Lionel Taylor told *Sportscope*. "He was still an amazing quarterback. He threw the kind of ball a man could move to. If a guy was running to his left, and covered, Frank would throw to the disadvantage side—to the right—and be on the money. Frank was not at his peak with the Broncos, but he still had a lot of snap on the ball. He was great at analyzing and anticipating defenses. With a solid team behind him, Frank would have shown the Bronco fans something."

"He was a strong leader who really wanted Denver to be a winner," said Jerry Sturm. "He led by example. Frank didn't hesitate to chew someone out in the huddle if the man wasn't doing his job. Frank didn't have a strong arm, but he was always accurate. He spent a lot of time helping our young quarterbacks."

A long-time Bronco fan added, "Tripper was smart, colorful, likeable and a great leader. With a few more points or a better defense, Frank would have brought us our first winning season and a division championship."

50

The football cliche that "a team is never any better than its quarterback" has been proven by the statistics. Between Tripucka's last game and Charley Johnson's first start Denver won 34 of 128 games—less than 30 percent. With Tripucka and Johnson calling signals the Broncos won almost 50 percent of their games.

Charley Johnson led New Mexico State to two Sun Bowl titles before being drafted by St. Louis as a future in 1960. "The Cardinals started building in 1962," recalled Charley. "By 1964 we were competitive, but in 1965 we had 19 major injuries—including me." Johnson was traded to Houston in 1970 and came to Denver two years later.

"Johnson is the all-time great leader," says Fred Gehrke. "The guys really work for him."

"He reads defenses as well as anyone in football," claims a teammate. "And this ability makes him one of the NFL's top quarterbacks."

Interviewing Charley Johnson is easy—once you find him. He is smart, sensitive and soft-spoken. After practice one afternoon Charley found a few minutes to sit in the shade and talk football.

"Since I started playing pro ball," he said, "The biggest change has been the defenses. They are more complex, much trickier and better disguised than 10 years ago."

"The quick release concept escapes me," Charley conceded. "There's no way to time it. What does it mean—how often you eat the ball? Some people say I have a quick release. Others say I'm too slow. I don't know."

"I like to throw a little less than half the time. It depends on how the game is going. Coach Coley calls all the plays here, but I can change them—audibolize—and I do about 70 percent of the time."

"I hate to throw interceptions," Charley admitted. "The other team almost always converts them to points. I'm very conscious of my ratio. I want to end up with more touchdown passes than interceptions."

Discussing Denver's past quarterback situation Johnson said, "It doesn't hurt to remove your starter once or twice. He can study the defense. That has helped me. But pulling a quarterback for a mistake or for no real reason is a negative thing. It puts extra pressure on the starter."

Charley's thoughts wandered back to the last Oakland game in 1973. "My wife and I were so sure we'd win," he said, "We made absolutely no plans to return to Houston. It wasn't until Monday that I realized the season was over."

Charley Johnson — "I've been fortunate during my football career. The people I've played with and for have never asked me to do more than I could do."

51

"At times back there you feel lonely and scared—there is nobody to sympathize with. I used to worry about calling the wrong play, but not anymore. With Ralston we think the next play will not only work, we think it will be the play that will win the game."

"I stayed down too long," he continued. "I've been hurt like that before and come back into the game. This time the team doctors felt I stayed down too long. I was very disappointed. We were moving when it happened and could have won the game. The whole team was very upset."

Johnson's medical records are as impressive as his passing statistics. He has suffered an unknown number of "mild" concussions, endured four broken collarbones and submitted to five knee operations. With all these injuries Charley could easily have quit football when Houston traded him in 1972.

"I went to Denver," Johnson said, "Because I thought I could help the Broncos. They've never had any stability at quarterback. I felt I could provide some."

The abundance of quarterbacks has helped determine Bronco history. Charley Johnson not only provided some stability, he ended Denver's long string of leaderless, losing seasons. With Johnson, Steve Ramsey and John Hufnagel, a new era of first-class, winning football is just beginning.

"The most important thing for any player—
not just a quarterback—is to learn his role
on the team. He must understand what
effect and importance he has, and how he
can help the team win. 'Never-wrong' types
cannot succeed in football. You must adjust
to situations and have the ability to honestly
evaluate what happened in a game."

DENVER'S TOP 10 QUARTERBACKS

Attempts		Completion Percentage		Interception Percentage		Touchdowns Per Pass		Yards Per Attempt	
Tripucka	1,277	Johnson	.546	Johnson	.048	Briscoe	.063	Johnson	7.51
Johnson	828	Tripucka	.518	Tensi	.055	Johnson	.057	Briscoe	7.09
Tensi	810	Lee	.513	Briscoe	.058	Tensi	.047	Ramsey	7.08
Slaughter	583	Horn	.508	McCormick	.059	Lee	.046	Lee	6.63
McCormick	537	Slaughter	.499	Liske	.062	Liske	.045	Tensi	6.36
Ramsey	416	Liske	.490	Lee	.066	Tripucka	.040	Slaughter	6.18
Liske	353	Ramsey	.481	Tripucka	.066	Slaughter	.038	Liske	6.18
Lee	343	Briscoe	.455	Slaughter	.067	Ramsey	.035	Horn	6.16
Briscoe	224	Tensi	.429	Ramsey	.071	McCormick	.032	Tripucka	5.98
Herring	223	McCormick	.368	Horn	.081	Horn	.017	McCormick	5.05

A COMPLETE STATISTICAL HISTORY OF DENVER'S QUARTERBACKS

Opponent	Quarterback(s)	Att.	Comp.	Int.	TDs	Net Yards	Result
1960							
at Boston	Tripucka	15	10	1	1	180	13-10 (W)
at Buffalo	Tripucka	26	14	2	2	156	27-21 (W)
at New York	Tripucka	29	14	1	1	214	24-28 (L)
Oakland	Tripucka	29	9	2	2	116	31-14 (W)
	Herring	9	4	0	0	59	
Los Angeles	Tripucka	32	16	2	0	155	19-23 (L)
Boston	Tripucka	37	20	2	4	287	31-24 (W)
Dallas	Tripucka	31	14	2	1	179	14-17 (L)
Houston	Tripucka	52	30	2	3	375	25-45 (L)
at Dallas	Tripucka	33	18	4	0	136	7-34 (L)
at Houston	Tripucka	52	26	2	1	268	10-20 (L)
Buffalo	Tripucka	41	19	5	3	338	38-38 (T)
New York	Tripucka	47	27	4	3	220	27-30 (L)
at Los Angeles	Tripucka	35	17	2	2	291	33-41 (L)
at Oakland	Tripucka	29	14	3	1	133	10-48 (L)
	Herring	13	5	1	0	78	

Opponent	Quarterback(s)	Att.	Comp.	Int.	TDs	Net Yards	Result
1961							
at Buffalo	Tripucka	19	11	1	1	94	22-10 (W)
	**Mingo	2	2	0	2	102	
	(**Tripucka to Mingo to Taylor)						
at Boston	Tripucka	49	20	0	2	206	17-45 (L)
at New York	Tripucka	31	18	0	1	110	28-35 (L)
	Herring	20	10	0	0	135	
at Oakland	Herring	24	13	1	1	168	19-33 (L)
	Tripucka	3	0	1	0	0	
Dallas	Tripucka	15	11	1	2	147	12-19 (L)
	Herring	10	4	2	0	62	
Oakland	Tripucka	24	14	2	1	191	27-24 (W)
	Herring	8	3	0	0	41	
New York	Tripucka	17	5	1	1	72	27-10 (W)
	Herring	20	12	2	2	133	
at San Diego	Tripucka	30	15	1	0	110	0-37 (L)
	Herring	15	6	3	0	124	
Houston	Tripucka	23	11	3	0	103	14-55 (L)
	Herring	24	9	1	0	68	
San Diego	Tripucka	49	23	5	1	285	16-19 (L)
Buffalo	Tripucka	25	11	4	0	69	10-23 (L)
	Herring	16	3	2	0	102	
at Houston	Herring	40	17	6	1	167	14-45 (L)
Boston	Tripucka	42	19	1	1	237	24-28 (L)
	Herring	6	3	2	0	20	
at Dallas	Tripucka	17	9	1	0	63	21-49 (L)
	Herring	28	13	3	1	140	
	(Taylor catches 100th pass of season; Filchock's last game)						
1962							
San Diego	Tripucka	47	28	2	2	376	30-21 (W)
	Enis	2	1	0	0	8	
at Buffalo	Tripucka	56	29	3	2	447	23-20 (W)
at Boston	Tripucka	47	22	2	1	275	16-41 (L)
	Shaw	9	5	0	1	174	
	(Shaw to Tarr for 97-yard TD—Broncos' longest scoring pass)						

55

Opponent	Quarterback(s)	Att.	Comp.	Int.	TDs	Net Yards	Result
at New York	Tripucka	29	20	3	1	242	32-10 (W
	Shaw	3	3	0	0	47	
Oakland	Shaw	25	9	4	0	137	44-7 (W
at Oakland	Tripucka	29	16	2	1	257	23-6 (W
	Shaw	3	0	1	0	0	
Houston	Tripucka	40	26	1	1	308	20-10 (W
Buffalo	Tripucka	20	12	2	5	168	38-45 (L
	Shaw	3	2	0	0	32	
at San Diego	Tripucka	32	17	1	1	202	23-20 (W
	Shaw	3	1	1	0	16	
Boston	Tripucka	26	10	1	1	89	29-33 (L
	Shaw	10	6	1	1	124	
Dallas	Tripucka	18	9	0	0	65	3-24 (L
	Shaw	11	4	0	0	35	
New York	Tripucka	15	9	2	1	113	45-46 (L
	Shaw	26	12	1	2	117	
at Houston	Tripucka	45	20	5	1	188	17-34 (L
	Shaw	7	1	3	0	5	
at Dallas	Tripucka	36	22	1	0	187	10-17 (L
	Shaw	10	6	3	0	96	

1963

Opponent	Quarterback(s)	Att.	Comp.	Int.	TDs	Net Yards	Result
Kansas City	Tripucka	4	1	2	0	3	7-59 (L
	Slaughter	31	14	3	1	135	

(Tripper's career fading fast—two of his first three passes are intercepted)

Opponent	Quarterback(s)	Att.	Comp.	Int.	TDs	Net Yards	Result
at Houston	Tripucka	11	6	3	0	28	14-20 (L
	Slaughter	11	5	0	0	73	

(Tripucka's last pro game)

Opponent	Quarterback(s)	Att.	Comp.	Int.	TDs	Net Yards	Result
Boston	Slaughter	18	7	2	0	109	14-10 (W
	McCormick	7	2	0	1	123	

(Slaughter hurt in third quarter)

Opponent	Quarterback(s)	Att.	Comp.	Int.	TDs	Net Yards	Result
San Diego	McCormick	36	18	1	3	265	50-34 (W
Houston	McCormick	8	2	0	0	9	24-33 (L
	Slaughter	24	13	5	2	245	

*(McCormick injures knee on a safety—does not play regularly
again until 1965)*

Opponent	Quarterback(s)	Att.	Comp.	Int.	TDs	Net Yards	Result
at Boston	Slaughter	11	7	0	1	133	21-40 (L
	Breaux	27	12	1	1	174	

Opponent	Quarterback(s)	Att.	Comp.	Int.	TDs	Net Yards	Result
at New York	Slaughter	21	11	0	3	179	35-35 (T)
	Breaux	11	5	1	0	37	
Buffalo	Slaughter	4	1	1	0	34	28-30 (L)
	Breaux	23	10	0	4	239	
	(Slaughter hurt in first quarter)						
at Buffalo	Breaux	17	9	1	0	62	17-27 (L)
	Slaughter	25	12	0	2	181	
New York	Slaughter	9	4	0	0	58	9-14 (L)
	McCormick	11	2	0	0	13	
Oakland	McCormick	10	2	2	0	7	10-26 (L)
	Breaux	22	14	1	1	180	
at Kansas City	Slaughter	34	18	2	1	244	21-52 (L)
at Oakland	Slaughter	35	20	0	2	298	31-35 (L)
	Breaux	7	4	1	0	51	
	(Slaughter hurt in second quarter)						
at San Diego	Breaux	31	16	2	1	193	20-58 (L)

1964

Opponent	Quarterback(s)	Att.	Comp.	Int.	TDs	Net Yards	Result
at New York	Lee	32	18	3	0	127	6-30 (L)
at Buffalo	Lee	32	13	2	1	168	13-30 (L)
	Slaughter	5	1	0	0	5	
Houston	Lee	32	17	2	0	239	17-38 (L)
	Slaughter	6	4	1	0	49	
Boston	Lee	10	5	1	0	44	10-39 (L)
	Slaughter	24	16	2	1	109	
	(Famous eight QB change game; Faulkner's last game)						
Kansas City	Lee	23	13	1	3	186	33-27 (W)
	(Mac Speedie's first pro win)						
at San Diego	Lee	32	16	2	2	100	14-42 (L)
at Oakland	Lee	22	13	2	0	171	7-40 (L)
	Slaughter	8	1	1	0	39	
at Kansas City	Slaughter	16	7	1	0	94	39-49 (L)
	Lee	17	9	1	2	213	
San Diego	Lee	23	12	3	0	171	20-31 (L)
New York	Lee	14	3	2	1	25	20-16 (W)
	Slaughter	7	4	0	0	19	

Opponent	Quarterback(s)	Att.	Comp.	Int.	TDs	Net Yards	Result
at Boston	Lee	23	11	1	1	121	7-12 (L)
	Slaughter	12	5	2	0	66	
Oakland	Slaughter	27	14	1	0	142	20-20 (T)
	Lee	3	1	0	0	16	
Buffalo	Slaughter	30	11	0	1	124	19-30 (L)
	Lee	1	1	0	1	30	
at Houston	Slaughter	53	34	3	1	283	15-34 (L)
	Lee	1	1	0	0	11	
	(Slaughter sets single-game Bronco completion record)						

1965

Opponent	Quarterback(s)	Att.	Comp.	Int.	TDs	Net Yards	Result
at San Diego	Slaughter	27	16	0	3	214	31-34 (L)
Buffalo	Slaughter	42	22	5	2	291	15-30 (L)
at Boston	Slaughter	9	3	2	0	19	27-10 (W)
	McCormick	15	8	0	0	55	
New York	McCormick	12	5	0	0	77	16-13 (W)
	Slaughter	20	13	1	0	106	
Kansas City	Slaughter	15	5	1	0	39	23-31 (L)
	McCormick	16	7	0	0	65	
Houston	McCormick	25	10	1	1	177	28-17 (W)
at Buffalo	McCormick	23	10	1	0	138	13-31 (L)
	Slaughter	17	10	0	1	137	
at New York	Slaughter	10	4	3	0	39	10-45 (L)
	McCormick	23	9	2	1	112	
San Diego	Slaughter	5	2	0	0	19	21-35 (L)
	McCormick	36	18	3	0	209	
	(Slaughter injures his shoulder)						
at Houston	McCormick	28	5	3	1	20	31-21 (W)
	(Denver intercepts six passes)						
Oakland	McCormick	36	13	4	1	200	20-28 (L)
	Lee	10	7	0	1	81	
at Oakland	Slaughter	2	0	0	0	0	13-24 (L)
	Lee	36	18	1	1	370	
	(Slaughter dislocates his other shoulder)						
Boston	Lee	35	19	2	3	239	20-28 (L)
	(Lee's last game; Taylor's 500th pro catch)						
at Kansas City	McCormick	37	18	0	3	232	35-45 (L)

Opponent	Quarterback(s)	Att.	Comp.	Int.	TDs	Net Yards	Result
1966							
at Houston	Slaughter	7	0	0	0	0	7-45 (L)
	McCormick	13	2	0	0	−1	
	("No-first-down" game)						
Boston	McCormick	25	10	3	1	120	10-24 (L)
	(Mac Speedie resigns)						
New York	McCormick	8	1	1	0	11	7-16 (L)
	Slaughter	18	7	0	1	124	
	(McCormick injured in second quarter; Slaughter's last game; Broncos hire Tobin Rote)						
Houston	McCormick	31	13	1	2	212	40-38 (W)
	(Ray Malavasi's first pro win)						
at Kansas City	McCormick	29	10	1	0	136	10-37 (L)
	Rote	6	2	1	0	28	
at Miami	McCormick	25	9	4	0	90	7-24 (L)
	Rote	2	1	0	0	12	
Kansas City	Choboian	31	17	4	1	204	10-56 (L)
	Glacken	2	1	0	0	15	
at San Diego	Choboian	13	6	0	0	71	17-24 (L)
	McCormick	18	9	0	0	91	
at Boston	Choboian	19	12	1	2	155	17-10 (W)
Oakland	Choboian	30	9	2	0	93	3-17 (L)
	McCormick	6	1	1	0	6	
San Diego	Choboian	25	12	1	0	173	20-17 (W)
	McCormick	1	0	1	0	0	
Miami	Choboian	25	14	2	1	273	17-7 (W)
at Oakland	Choboian	20	12	2	0	141	10-28 (L)
	Glacken	6	4	0	1	54	
at Buffalo	Glacken	3	1	0	0	15	21-38 (L)
	McCormick	37	13	3	3	328	
	(Malavasi's last game as head coach)						
1967							
Boston	Tensi	19	8	0	2	145	26-21 (W)
	(Denver intercepts six passes)						
at Oakland	Tensi	12	2	1	0	17	0-51 (L)
	Glacken	4	0	0	0	0	

Opponent	Quarterback(s)	Att.	Comp.	Int.	TDs	Net Yards	Result
at Miami	Tensi	20	6	2	0	55	21-35 (L
New York	Tensi	30	14	1	2	256	24-38 (L
at Houston	Tensi	22	6	3	0	58	6-10 (L
Buffalo	Leclair	17	9	0	1	114	16-17 (L
	Tensi	2	2	0	0	45	
San Diego	Tensi	36	15	0	2	234	21-33 (L
at Kansas City	Tensi	19	7	2	1	155	9-52 (L
	Leclair	15	7	1	0	103	
Oakland	Tensi	15	5	1	1	97	17-21 (L
	Leclair	6	2	0	0	50	

(Denver QBs sacked 11 times for 95 yards lost)

Opponent	Quarterback(s)	Att.	Comp.	Int.	TDs	Net Yards	Result
Houston	Leclair	7	1	0	0	8	18-20 (L
	Tensi	32	13	0	2	156	
at Buffalo	Tensi	33	14	2	2	190	21-20 (W
at San Diego	Tensi	41	18	2	2	253	20-24 (L
at New York	Tensi	16	7	0	1	59	33-24 (W
Kansas City	Tensi	28	14	3	1	195	24-38 (L

1968

Opponent	Quarterback(s)	Att.	Comp.	Int.	TDs	Net Yards	Result
at Cincinnati	McCormick	19	8	1	0	89	10-24 (L
	Leclair	12	6	0	1	82	

(John McCormick's last game)

Opponent	Quarterback(s)	Att.	Comp.	Int.	TDs	Net Yards	Result
at Kansas City	Leclair	25	16	3	0	227	2-34 (L
	DiVito	5	1	0	0	16	
Boston	Leclair	17	5	2	0	92	17-20 (L
	Briscoe	6	2	0	0	43	

(Jim Leclair's last game)

Opponent	Quarterback(s)	Att.	Comp.	Int.	TDs	Net Yards	Result
Cincinnati	Briscoe	11	4	0	0	37	10-7 (W
	Tensi	22	9	0	1	84	
at New York	Tensi	22	10	0	1	201	21-13 (W
at San Diego	Tensi	14	6	1	0	84	24-55 (L
	Briscoe	30	17	2	3	237	

(Tensi removed after interception in second quarter)

Opponent	Quarterback(s)	Att.	Comp.	Int.	TDs	Net Yards	Result
Miami	Tensi	9	1	3	0	13	21-14 (W
	Briscoe	13	7	0	0	114	

(Briscoe runs for two touchdowns)

Opponent	Quarterback(s)	Att.	Comp.	Int.	TDs	Net Yards	Result
Boston	Tensi	17	11	1	2	206	35-14 (W)
	Briscoe	2	1	1	0	26	
Oakland	Tensi	27	10	2	1	81	7-43 (L)
	Briscoe	9	1	1	0	7	
Houston	Tensi	8	1	1	0	40	17-38 (L)
	Briscoe	19	9	1	1	119	
(Tensi breaks his collarbone)							
Buffalo	Briscoe	29	12	2	4	335	34-32 (W)
San Diego	Briscoe	33	15	0	3	218	23-47 (L)
Oakland	Briscoe	41	15	4	2	251	27-33 (L)
Kansas City	Briscoe	31	10	2	1	202	7-30 (L)
	DiVito	1	0	0	0	0	
(DiVito and Briscoe's last game; first game in newly-named Mile High Stadium)							

1969

Opponent	Quarterback(s)	Att.	Comp.	Int.	TDs	Net Yards	Result
Boston	Tensi	15	10	0	3	205	26-21 (W)
New York	Tensi	4	1	1	0	21	21-19 (W)
	Liske	20	11	1	2	138	
(Tensi hurts his right knee)							
Buffalo	Liske	45	17	5	3	289	28-41 (L)
(Liske sacked five times)							
Kansas City	Tensi	8	2	0	0	12	13-26 (L)
	Liske	22	13	1	1	149	
Oakland	Tensi	34	12	2	1	130	14-24 (L)
Cincinnati	Tensi	14	7	0	2	149	30-23 (W)
	Liske	1	0	1	0	0	
(Little rushes for 166 yards; Denver sacks Bengal QBs 10 times)							
Houston	Tensi	32	14	0	1	243	21-24 (L)
San Diego	Tensi	32	15	2	1	219	13-0 (W)
(Denver's first shutout; Broncos sack Charger QBs six times)							
Oakland	Tensi	36	19	1	0	214	10-41 (L)
Houston	Tensi	21	7	1	1	134	20-20 (T)
San Diego	Tensi	26	19	1	3	301	24-45 (L)
	Liske	10	7	2	0	62	
Kansas City	Tensi	33	12	2	0	179	17-31 (L)

Opponent	Quarterback(s)	Att.	Comp.	Int.	TDs	Net Yards	Result
at Miami	Tensi	31	13	2	2	183	24-27 (L)
Cincinnati	Liske	17	13	1	3	207	27-16 (W)

1970

Opponent	Quarterback(s)	Att.	Comp.	Int.	TDs	Net Yards	Result
at Buffalo	Liske	11	4	1	0	52	25-10 (W)
	Tensi	14	4	0	1	108	
Pittsburgh	Liske	11	4	0	0	38	16-13 (W)
	Tensi	14	8	2	1	140	
Kansas City	Liske	25	15	0	1	135	26-13 (W)
	(Denver sacks Chief QB seven times and intercepts three passes)						
at Oakland	Liske	32	17	1	1	188	23-35 (L)
Atlanta	Liske	33	19	0	1	156	24-10 (W)
at San Francisco	Liske	17	8	2	1	103	14-19 (L)
	Tensi	9	3	1	0	18	
Washington	Liske	25	9	1	0	86	3-19 (L)
	Tensi	8	5	2	0	37	
at San Diego	Tensi	22	14	1	1	170	21-24 (L)
Oakland	Tensi	13	4	2	0	66	19-24 (L)
	Liske	25	10	1	1	152	
	(Steve Tensi's last game)						
at New Orleans	Liske	26	15	1	2	262	31-6 (W)
	Pastrana	5	2	0	0	42	
at Houston	Liske	16	5	2	0	73	21-31 (L)
	Pastrana	15	4	1	1	98	
at Kansas City	Pastrana	21	9	5	0	115	0-16 (L)
San Diego	Pastrana	8	4	0	0	49	17-17 (T)
	Liske	17	6	2	0	95	
	(Pete Liske's last game)						
Cleveland	Pastrana	26	10	3	0	116	13-27 (L)
	(Al Pastrana's last game)						

1971

Opponent	Quarterback(s)	Att.	Comp.	Int.	TDs	Net Yards	Result
Miami	Horn	20	11	1	1	118	10-10 (T)
	(Famous "half-a-loaf" game)						
at Green Bay	Horn	33	16	6	0	186	13-34 (L)
	Ramsey	8	7	0	1	69	

62

Opponent	Quarterback(s)	Att.	Comp.	Int.	TDs	Net Yards	Result
Kansas City	Horn	27	14	4	0	168	3-16 (L)
Oakland	Horn	8	5	0	0	131	16-27 (L)
	Ramsey	16	6	2	1	98	

(Horn hurts his left Achilles tendon late in second quarter)

San Diego	Horn	17	7	1	0	71	20-16 (W)
t Cleveland	Horn	16	8	0	1	85	27-0 (W)
t Philadelphia	Horn	27	13	2	0	138	16-17 (L)

(Horn sacked three times; Broncos lose four fumbles)

Detroit	Horn	20	13	0	1	164	20-24 (L)
Cincinnati	Horn	5	1	0	0	6	10-24 (L)
	Ramsey	13	6	1	1	106	

(Horn separates his right shoulder, will not play again for Denver; Lou Saban resigns, leaving Jerry Smith in charge for last five games)

t Kansas City	Ramsey	37	17	3	0	231	10-28 (L)
t Pittsburgh	Ramsey	25	14	1	0	161	22-10 (W)

(Denver defense sacks Steeler QBs four times and recovers five fumbles)

Chicago	Ramsey	16	8	2	0	81	6-3 (W)

(Broncos sack Bobby Douglass nine times)

t San Diego	Ramsey	25	10	3	1	169	17-45 (L)
t Oakland	Ramsey	37	16	1	1	205	13-21 (L)

(Jerry Smith's last game as head coach; Floyd Little rushes 79 yards to capture NFL title)

1972

Opponent	Quarterback(s)	Att.	Comp.	Int.	TDs	Net Yards	Result
Houston	Ramsey	24	11	1	1	261	30-17 (W)
San Diego	Ramsey	25	14	3	0	192	14-37 (L)
	Johnson	12	6	3	0	66	
Kansas City	Ramsey	35	13	3	1	247	24-45 (L)
Cincinnati	Ramsey	14	6	0	0	86	10-21 (L)
	Johnson	5	0	0	0	0	
Minnesota	Ramsey	5	3	1	0	11	20-23 (L)
	Johnson	22	12	1	1	164	
Oakland	Johnson	28	20	0	2	361	30-23 (W)
Cleveland	Johnson	24	14	1	2	140	20-27 (L)
N. Y. Giants	Johnson	24	11	3	0	126	17-29 (L)

(Johnson sacked four times)

Los Angeles	Johnson	23	11	2	1	121	16-10 (W)

Opponent	Quarterback(s)	Att.	Comp.	Int.	TDs	Net Yards	Result
Oakland	Johnson	31	16	1	2	178	20-37 (L)
at Atlanta	Johnson	7	5	0	0	113	20-23 (L)
	Ramsey	18	9	0	1	116	
	(Johnson suffers a mild concussion in the second quarter)						
at Kansas City	Johnson	35	18	2	1	211	21-24 (L)
	(Johnson sacked four times and Denver loses four fumbles)						
San Diego	Johnson	10	6	1	2	85	38-13 (W)
	(Nine degree weather; Denver defense recovers five fumbles and intercepts two passes)						
New England	Johnson	17	13	0	3	218	45-21 (W)
	Ramsey	10	7	0	0	113	
	Ernst	4	1	0	0	10	

1973

Opponent	Quarterback(s)	Att.	Comp.	Int.	TDs	Net Yards	Result
Cincinnati	Johnson	25	11	1	0	190	28-10 (W)
San Francisco	Johnson	35	16	5	2	212	34-36 (L)
Chicago	Johnson	39	24	2	1	295	14-33 (L)
at Kansas City	Johnson	19	10	1	1	120	14-16 (L)
at Houston	Johnson	20	9	0	4	202	48-20 (W)
	(Johnson becomes 18th QB to pass for 20,000 yards)						
Oakland	Johnson	24	11	2	0	115	23-23 (T)
at N. Y. Jets	Johnson	17	11	0	2	137	40-28 (W)
	Ramsey	5	3	0	1	115	
	(Johnson injures his knee in the third quarter)						
at St. Louis	Johnson	24	15	1	1	205	17-17 (T)
San Diego	Johnson	29	16	1	2	234	30-19 (W)
at Pittsburgh	Johnson	20	13	0	1	86	23-13 (W)
Kansas City	Johnson	21	10	1	2	144	14-10 (W)
Dallas	Johnson	27	12	1	1	175	10-22 (L)
	Ramsey	3	1	0	0	15	
at San Diego	Johnson	26	15	0	2	216	42-28 (W)
	(This game assures the Broncos of their first winning season in history)						
at Oakland	Johnson	22	11	1	1	91	17-21 (L)
	Ramsey	16	4	2	1	54	
	(Johnson suffers a mild concussion in the fourth quarter)						

Opponent	Quarterback(s)	Att.	Comp.	Int.	TDs	Net Yards	Result
1974							
Los Angeles	Johnson	26	13	0	1	144	10-17 (L)
Pittsburgh	Johnson	15	6	1	2	129	35-35 (T)
	Ramsey	12	6	1	2	62	
t Washington	Johnson	22	11	0	0	112	3-30 (L)
	Ramsey	2	1	1	0		
t Kansas City	Johnson	7	1	2	0	34	17-14 (W)
	Ramsey	9	4	0	0	63	
New Orleans	Ramsey	27	17	2	2	295	33-17 (W)
	Hufnagel	0	0	0	0	0	
San Diego	Johnson	12	9	0	1	146	27-7 (W)
	Van Heusen	1	1	0	0	41	
t Cleveland	Johnson	27	14	0	2	207	21-23 (L)
Oakland	Johnson	24	13	1	2	240	17-28 (L)
t Baltimore	Johnson	16	9	0	1	60	17-6 (W)
Kansas City	Johnson	42	28	2	2	445	34-42 (L)
	Hufnagel	7	4	0	0	46	
t Oakland	Johnson	7	4	0	0	76	20-17 (W)
	Ramsey	11	5	1	1	59	
t Detroit	Johnson	22	12	1	1	130	31-27 (W)
Houston	Johnson	21	15	1	1	219	37-24 (W)
t San Diego	Ramsey	13	8	2	0	94	0-17 (L)
	Johnson	3	2	0	0	28	
	Hufnagel	3	2	0	0	24	

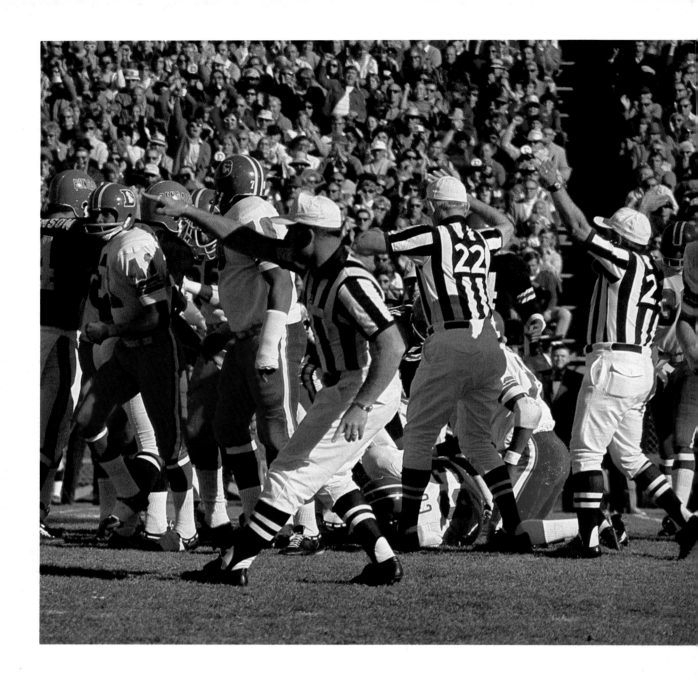

A GAME WITHOUT PLAYERS

Football games have been played without footballs, field goals, rules, stopwatches, coaches, owners, unions, dicker rods, traffic jams, season tickets, Howard Cosell, protective equipment, quick kicks, marching bands, goal posts, point spreads, Astrodomes and Super Bowls. But you cannot play a game without players...

Frank Filchock

Gene Mingo

Frank Filchock's players, the first Broncos, were a collection of CFL and NFL castoffs, walk-ons, unsung rookies and free agents. Aging veterans dusted off their credentials and joined enthusiastic unknowns at training camp in Golden. Filchock and Dean Griffing drafted, courted, cajoled and coaxed players out of retirement to assemble a team. The first Broncos deserve special praise and credit. They played without success, security or substantial financial reward— doing the best they could with what they were.

Although Denver led the 1960 AFL in losses, three Broncos won important individual honors. Goose Gonsoulin led the league in interceptions. Lionel Taylor started his string of pass-catching crowns. And Gene Mingo, pro football's first black placekicking specialist, put together six touchdowns, 18 field goals and 33 conversions for 123 points and the first AFL scoring title. His 137 points in 1962 also led the league.

Mingo, an Akron, Ohio, baseball star, spurned college scholarships and offers from the Baltimore Orioles and Pittsburgh Pirates to join the Navy.

Mingo was considered one of the best all-around halfbacks in the early AFL. He could run, pass and kick. As a runner and passer, Gene had a superb sense of balance. He kick with a smooth, seemingly effortless style--was deadly on extra points and long field goal but inconsistent on middle-distance kicks.

"I became a mess cook," Gene old *Sportscope.* "That's how I tarted playing football. We sed to bake our own bread and ne day we were goofing round using a loaf for a football. The head cook caught us nd chewed us out. He got me a ryout on the base team."

After Mingo's discharge he eturned to Akron. When the AFL was formed, Gene wrote Dean Griffing, asking for a tryut. The Bronco GM had seen Mingo play at Norfolk so he nvited the big running back to amp. Mingo's Bronco career asted five years. He then played or Oakland, Miami, Washington, New Orleans and Pittsburgh efore retiring in 1969.

Mingo admitted that carrying he ball in the early Bronco ears was less than delightful. The limited success Gene and ther runners enjoyed was made ossible by three Bronco lockers—Ken Adamson, Eldon Danenhauer and Jerry Sturm.

Adamson came to Denver after a rilliant career at Notre Dame. He aptained the Irish during his enior year. Danenhauer attended somewhat less famous college— tate Teachers in Pittsburg, Kansas. Sturm played fullback, ffensive guard, tackle and center t his alma mater, the University f Illinois. In the early years this io gave strength to an otherwise eak offensive line.

Danenhauer gave 150 percent," teammate recalled. "He lacked per speed and quickness, but ad everything else—size, desire, ntelligence, leadership. He tried ery hard, made it a point to arn all the offensive positions. ldon kept us together those rst few years."

When I graduated," Danenauer wrote in a 1961 eport, "I was approached by couts from both pro leagues. I ad looked forward to trying he game for a few years and ave a lot of thought to my noice of clubs.

Gordie Holz, Eldon Danenhauer and Jack Mattox

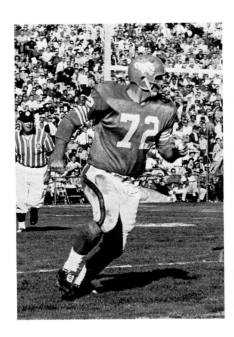

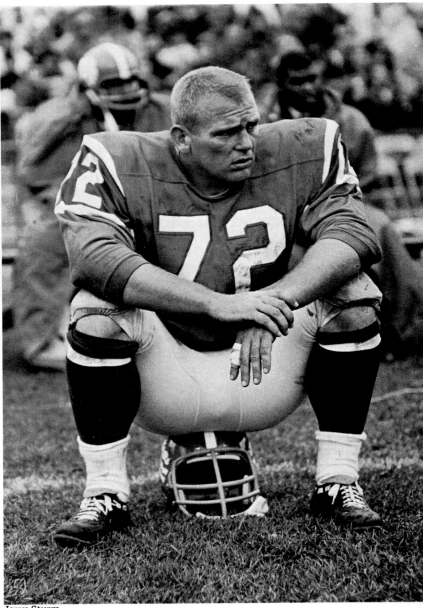

Jerry Sturm

"I signed with Denver for several reasons. Primarily, the Broncos were a new club in a new league and I would be starting fairly even with the rest of the players. As a rookie, this was an important consideration. Another reason I chose Denver was that I like this part of the country. The West is wide open for business opportunities and I felt that if I established myself with the Broncos, the contacts and publicity would open some business career for me. And I was right.

"My brother Bill and I came together. Bill did not make the team but his background with the club helped him find a job in Denver."

After six seasons in Denver, Lou Saban sent Jerry Sturm to New Orleans in 1967. Jerry played for the Saints, Oilers and Eagles before retiring in 1972. Sturm combined versatility with size, speed, desire and determination.

"Jerry is one of the nicest guys you will ever meet," said John McCormick, quickly adding, *off the field*. For a man his size it's amazing how many sports Jerry excels in. He was a genuine all-around-athlete."

Chuck Gavin

While Adamson, Danenhauer and Sturm tried to plug Denver's sieve-like offensive line, lanky Austin "Goose" Gonsoulin performed defensive magic in the Bronco secondary.

"Gonsoulin had total intelligence of the game," said Fred Gehrke. "Today's coaches might think he was too slow to play safety, but his football knowledge made up for his lack of speed."

Gonsoulin, Baylor's defensive team captain, played seven seasons for Denver, including a starting role in the Broncos' first 61 games. Goose contributed to Denver's fast start in 1960 with a game-saving interception at Boston on opening day and by picking off four Buffalo aeriels the following week in a 27-21 Bronco victory.

Many of Gonsoulin's interceptions resulted from the relentless pass rush of Charles Gavin, Bud McFadin and Wahoo McDaniel. Gavin, a Tennessee State star, spent two years in the CFL before coming to Denver. A juvenile counselor in the off season, Gavin was sidelined in 1960 by an ankle injury, but returned the following year to help McFadin pressure opposing passers.

Goose Gonsoulin

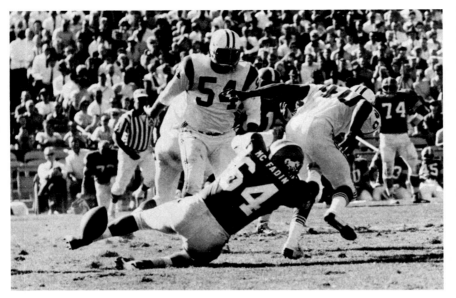

McFadin (280 pounds) may not remember rolling over the Broncos' rookie photographer (170 pounds) in 1962. But the photographer (Dick Burnell) still remembers.

McFadin, a left-handed, ex-Longhorn, threw enemy blockers off balance with his opposite-hand stance and charge. McFadin's pro career included five years at Los Angeles, four years at Denver and two seasons with Houston.

"McFadin was an *intimidating* person," said a teammate. "He was a big man—in stature, reputation and professional experience. He knew so much football, it was like having an extra coach out on the field. I can still see him chewing that big wad of tobacco."

One of Denver's most colorful defensemen was Ed "Wahoo" McDaniel. The ex-Sooner linebacker spent nine years in pro football, playing for the Oilers, Broncos, Jets and Dolphins before devoting his full time to professional wrestling, fishing and hunting. McDaniel battled the scale for most of his football career. Possibly because of his weight problem, Wahoo was considered much more effective against the run than the pass.

No doubt McDaniel dreaded covering Lionel Taylor in Bronco passing drills. Most early AFL offenses emphasized the pass. Lionel Taylor emphasized the catch.

The crafty receiver caught 543 passes for 6,875 yards during his seven seasons with Denver. He won the AFL receiving crown five times with average speed, good moves, and what some considered the best hands in pro football. Lionel could also shake loose for extra yardage after making one of his patented circus catches.

"Wahoo" McDaniel

80

Two great receivers—Mac Speedie congratulates Lionel Taylor after Lionel's 500th reception on December 12, 1965.

Taylor spent hours practicing those catches. He always seemed to have a football in his hands—on and off the field. Cut by the Chicago Bears, Taylor reported to Denver, caught seven passes and scored two touchdowns in the Broncos' home opener in 1960, a 31-14 victory over Oakland. Lionel's teammates describe him as a man with overwhelming confidence and pride; a team man; and a natural leader.

Gene Prebola

John McCormick hands off to the Broncos leading rusher in 1961—Don Stone

In 1961 Taylor teamed with Gene Prebola, providing the Broncos with a pair of receiving threats. Prebola, from Boston University, brought impressive credentials—33 receptions for 404 yards and two TDs—from Oakland to Denver. Mingo, Prebola, Taylor and three running backs—Al Carmichael, Al Frazier and Don Stone—accounted for most of Denver's offense during the Filchock years.

As a Packer Carmichael made NFL history on October 7, 1956, when he returned a kickoff 106 yards for a touchdown against the Bears.

In Denver's first game Al raced 59 yards with Frank Tripucka's swing pass for a touchdown. A TV and movie stunt man in his spare time, Carmichael suffered a broken leg after eight 1960 games. He had compiled 1,509 total yards before his injury. A fast, deceptive runner, Carmichael's two years with Denver followed a six-year stint at Green Bay and an outstanding collegiate career at USC.

In 1961 Denver signed Florida A&M track star Al "Scooter" Frazier and Razorback runner Don Stone. Stone led the Broncos in rushing in 1961. He left the Broncos after the 1965 season and played a year each

Al Frazier

with Buffalo and Houston. During his three years with Denver, Frazier used changing speeds and smooth, swift movements to gain yardage.

Filchock's Broncos, a hodgepodge of excellent athletes and players long since forgotten, compiled a two-year record of 7-20-1. More than 160,000 home-town fans endured the team's first two seasons. Most of them were probably happy when Frank was fired in December, 1961, but it is highly unlikely any coach could have done much better. The early Broncos lacked organization, depth and consistency.

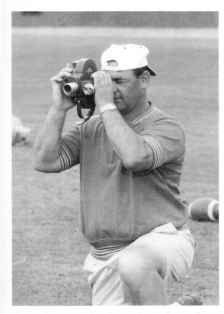

Denver's second head coach—Jack Faulkner

Jim Fraser

For half a season Jack Faulkner fielded a horse of a different color. With new coaches, new uniforms and a few new faces, the 1962 Broncos won six of their first seven games. The remainder of Faulkner's coaching career at Denver was filled with failure and frustration.

Hank Stram believes, "kicking can decide four to six games per season." Most pro coaches agree. In 1962 Denver started assembling a continuing crew of powerful punters. Former para- trooper Jim Fraser led the AFL in punting from 1962 through 1964. The ex-Badger doubled as a linebacker until he was traded to Kansas City in 1965. Fraser played for the Chiefs, Patriots and Saints before leaving foot- ball in 1968.

Charger castoff Bob Scarpitto also joined the Broncos in 1962. Bob led the league in 1966-67, setting an AFL record in 1967 with 105 punts. He was traded to Boston in 1968 and burnt his old teammates with a career-high 87-yard punt when the Patriots visited Denver in September.

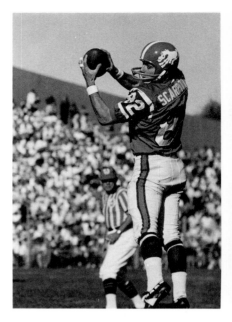

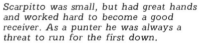

Scarpitto was small, but had great hands and worked hard to become a good receiver. As a punter he was always a threat to run for the first down.

A sociology major at Notre Dame, the small, versatile "Scraps" also caught a few passes for the Broncos.

"He was extremely dangerous after making a catch," said Mac Speedie. "Bob's very quick reactions helped him develop into a fine receiver."

Scarpitto's speed was an inside joke in the AFL. "Everybody thought I was slow," Bob once commented, "until I ran by them and caught the ball."

Another seemingly undersized Bronco was Colorado University's Bob McCullough.

"I came in as a linebacker," Bob recalled. "One day an offensive guard quit right in the middle of scrimmage. Coach Martin looked at the defense, pointed at me, mispronounced my name and stuck me in at guard. I played there the next four years."

Bob Zeman

Bob McCullough

"Most of the NFL veterans were not that anxious to help an AFL rookie. Not Bud McFadin—he took the time to teach me how to play offense in the pros."

Ray Jacobs

Had McCullough stayed on defense he would have teamed with Bob Zeman, Ray Jacobs and Willie Brown, three Bronco newcomers during the Faulkner years.

San Diego sold Zeman in 1962 and in his first year as a Bronco, Bob joined Goose Gonsoulin on the AFL All-Star team. Zeman quit playing football in 1966 and has since coached at Northwestern, Wisconsin—his alma mater, and with the Oakland Raiders.

In 1963 the Broncos acquired Ray Jacobs, a defensive tackle from Howard Payne, and Willie Brown from the Houston Oilers.

Willie Brown

Brown, an intelligent, all-around athlete intercepted nine passes in 1964 and was voted to the AFL All-Star team. He was bothered by injuries in 1965 and traded to Oakland the following year. Brown developed into one of the best football players Denver ever released.

harlie Mitchell

In 1963 Denver signed three potential super running backs— Billy Joe from Villanova, Hewritt Dixon from Florida A&M, and Charlie Mitchell from the University of Washington. Mitchell, Tom Janik and Tom Nomina were the first future Broncos to play in the College All-Star game in Chicago.

Billy Joe

Hewritt Dixon

Dixon, a strong, hard-running fullback, played three seasons for Denver before being traded to Oakland. During Dixon's Bronco career a quarterback complained, "We couldn't call audibles with Hewritt in there. He could never remember our system."

The Broncos' 1963 backfield also included Billy Joe. Joe was voted the most valuable player in both the 1962 Sun Bowl and 1963 Liberty Bowl. As a pro Billy's 649 yards earned him Rookie of the Year honors in 1963. Billy and his famous bunions journeyed to Buffalo in 1965 in exchange for another pretty fair running back— Carlton Gilchrist.

Before his sudden departure in 1964 Jack Faulkner brought four more talented footballers to Denver. John Griffin, a defensive halfback from Memphis State, was purchased from the Rams. Griffin gained fame the following year when he scored two touchdowns against Houston—one on an interception and another on a blocked punt.

The Broncos bolstered their offensive line by drafting Texas A&M star Ray Kubala. Ray, a big, hard-working, dependable tackle and center, played four years at Denver.

1963 was a good year for running backs and 1964 was the season for receivers. The Broncos obtained Odell Barry, an end from Findley, and converted him into a punt and kickoff return specialist. In 1964 Odell set a dubious AFL record with 47 kickoff returns.

"Slaughter and I took Ray out drinking one night," reminisced John McCormick. "We were drinking beer and whiskey. The bartender was pouring straight stuff for Kubala and slipping shots of coke to Mickey and me. That big _____ drank us under the table anyway."

Barry left football for medical reasons but stayed in sports. He became very successful in Northglenn's recreation department.

Barry, Lionel Taylor, Bob Scarpitto and the rest of the receiving corps were joined by Al Denson, another fine athlete from Florida A&M. Denson could leap tall buildings, was a good blocker, and a fast, deceptive runner. He enjoyed four good seasons until 1968 when he broke his collarbone *twice*. In 1970 Al was traded to Minnesota where he played a year before retiring.

The Broncos added several quality athletes during the Faulkner years. After a 6-1 start Denver finished 7-7 in 1962; 2-11-1 in 1963; and were 0-4 in 1964 when Jack was fired. Although the Broncos improved during Faulkner's reign, they obviously did not make significant progress in relation to the rest of the league.

Al Denson, as they say, had all the tools. But he seemed more interested in using them to build his own monument than helping the Broncos succeed as a team.

Ray Malavasi, Mac Speedie, Gerald Phipps, Allan Phipps

Larry Kaminski

Mac Speedie's era included several important external and internal events. The NBC-AFL agreement led to the AFL-NFL merger. The Phipps brothers bought Empire Sports. Season ticket sales soared. And the Broncos acquired a ton of talented players.

With an impressive number of good athletes wearing Bronco uniforms, Speedie and interim coach Ray Malavasi posted an unimpressive 10-27-1 record through 1966. Why the influx of promising players did not derail Denver's plunge into the loss column is still an unanswered question.

Lee Bernet, Bob Breitenstein, Larry Kaminski and Bob Young became Bronco offensive linemen—perhaps the hardest position in football. Blockers must fire out and hit, slant and angle, pull and lead, screen and shield—all against a wide variety of moving targets.

Tackles Lee Bernet, twice voted to the All-Big Ten *scholastic* team at the University of Wisconsin, and Bob Breitenstein, All-Missouri Valley Conference at Tulsa, flanked Larry Kaminski at center.

Kaminski, All-Big Ten at Purdue, made the team without exceptional size or speed. He

worked hard, became a good blocker and delivered consistently solid performances.

"Every year," an ex-coach commented, "Larry was challenged by bigger, faster rookies. When the training and pre-season ended, there he would be again at starting center."

Wendell Hayes

Abner Haynes (28) came to Denver in a trade with Kansas City for Jim Fraser. He scored 21 touchdowns in 1962 as a Dallas Texan. Wendell Hayes (29) joined the Broncos as a free agent after unsuccessful tryouts with Dallas and Oakland. He was the 10th best AFL rusher in 1965.

The Bronco backfield kept getting bigger and better. North Texas State's Abner Haynes; Humboldt State's Wendell Hayes; and Cookie Gilchrist all came to Denver during the Speedie years. The arrival and abilities of Haynes and Hayes

were almost lost in the ceremony and controversy surrounding Gilchrist's Bronco career.

"I would rather retire than play in Denver, "Cookie told the *Denver Post.* It was nothing personal, he explained, just a matter of money.

"Gilchrist was the ultimate in a running, blocking fullback," said Fred Gehrke. "He would over-shadow Csonka if he played on a team with Miami's blocking."

Mac Speedie put it very simply—"He was the best football player in the AFL."

Several of Gilchrist's teammates agreed. "He was a magnificent player," said one. "Once on the field, Cookie worked hard and played with great pride. He gave 100 percent; was a great blocker; and a natural leader. It was a pleasure to play on the same team with him."

Gilchrist led the AFL in rushing in 1962 and 1964 with Buffalo. He came to Denver in 1965, played for Miami in 1966, returned to Denver in 1967, and retired in 1968. He served the Broncos as a special consultant before drifting away from football. Gilchrist is reportedly working on *Kings Sometimes Walk While Slaves Ride Great White Horses,* an autobiography. It should be worth reading.

Gilchrist blocked so hard you could hear pads cracking in the stands. He also drove a hard bargain at contract time. Cookie was friendly and articulate—quick to sign a fan's program or chat with a reporter.

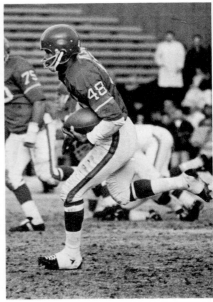

Nemiah Wilson, nicknamed "Tricky" or "Speedy", was one of the smallest defensive backs in the league at 170 pounds, but he could bring down the biggest, strongest runners. Wilson became a bona fide superstar after leaving Denver.

A flock of defensive specialists came to Denver during Speedie's years: Tackles Jerry Inman and Bill Keating; linebackers Arch Matsos and John Bramlett; and backs Goldie Sellers and Nemiah Wilson.

Sellers, who intercepted 19 passes in his last two years at Grambling, doubled as a Bronco kickoff returner. Wilson, also from Grambling, thrilled Denver fans with his interceptions and open-field running until Saban sent him to Oakland in 1968.

Michigan State's Arch Matsos was an AFL All-Star in 1960-61 with Buffalo and in 1963 with Oakland. He ended his career in 1966 with Denver and San Diego. John "Bull" Bramlett was a football and baseball letterman at Memphis State. He played minor league baseball for two years at Tulsa, where he earned his nickname chasing a foul ball through a fence.

Goldie Sellers

Eric Crabtree

In 1965 "Bull" sacked opposing quarterbacks at least once in seven consecutive games. He placed second in the AFL Rookie of the Year balloting. Bramlett left Denver in 1967 and played for Miami, Boston and Atlanta before retiring in 1971. Eric Crabtree, Jerry Inman and Bill Keating also became Broncos in 1966. Crabtree, drafted as a defensive back, developed into an excellent pass receiver and kickoff return specialist. Inman attended Boise Junior College for two years before entering the University of Oregon. He was a Little All-American at Boise and All-Coast at Oregon. Michigan's Bill Keating played two years in Denver before being traded to Miami. An injury to Bill's brother Tom, in an AFL All-Star game, prompted the new league to rectify an oversight. Their insurance coverage did not include All-Star games.

Jerry Inman

Colorful "Bull" Bramlett stretches to deflect a Parelli pass. "He played with reckless abandon," a teammate stated.

Ray Malavasi

Lou Saban

After two games in 1966 Mac Speedie submitted to the pressures associated with losing. Ray Malavasi completed the season while Denver's continually growing legion of fans hopefully waited for a coach to lead the Broncos to victory.

Lou Saban was the first Bronco head coach to participate in the unified AFL-NFL draft. Coaches and owners, weary of high-cost bidding wars, liked the new system. The players were not as happy. They not only lost their bargaining power, they could possibly be drafted by a team they did not particularly care to play for.

Denver was one such team. Melvin Durslag, a syndicated Los Angeles columnist, wrote about a UCLA star who narrowly missed being drafted by the Broncos. Durslag described "a man who had just endured a harrowing experience" and added, "Why in football has Denver come to symbolize Siberia? Denver is a good town with clean air, broad streets and a healthy attitude on nudity."

Saban's 1967 accomplishments alone had tremendous impact on the Denver Broncos. He moved the team to new administrative and practice facilities. He signed Floyd Little—the first number one draft choice to ink a Bronco contract. And in pre-season, he coached the first AFL victory over an NFL team beating Detroit 13-7.

Dave Costa

With Little, Dave Costa, Rich Jackson, Chip Myrtle, Pete Duranko, George Goeddeke, Mike Current and Fran Lynch became Broncos in 1967.

All-WAC at Utah, Costa started his AFL career in 1963 with Oakland. He was runner-up Rookie of the Year. Dave spent a year at Buffalo before coming to Denver. Despite asthma and flat feet as a New York youngster, Costa played quarterback in high school. Dave was traded to San Diego in 1972 after a training camp dispute with John Ralston.

ich Jackson

hip Myrtle

Also released by Ralston was Baton Rouge ex-deputy sheriff Rich Jackson. "Rich was as good a defensive player as you will ever find," said Fred Gehrke. "He had some problems off the field, but was a complete, dedicated player once he took the field."

Linebacker Chip Myrtle was one of the many players Saban coached at Maryland and brought to Denver. Lou was no longer a Bronco in 1972 when Chip enjoyed his best year with 31 tackles and 17 assists.

Saban did see Notre Dame's Pete Duranko develop into an All-Pro. Pete is big, fast, smart and versatile. "But not mean enough," said Gehrke. "If Duranko was mean, there is no telling what he could do. He apologizes and picks guys up after tackling them." Pete missed the 1971 season with a knee injury, but came back strong in 1973 with five sacks and 58 tackles.

The first four 1967 draft choices were Floyd Little, Pete Duranko, George Goeddeke and Mike Current. None of the 25 other pro teams fared better. Goeddeke, Duranko's teammate at Notre Dame, can play tackle, guard or center. George was All-Pro in 1969. A knee injury sidelined him in 1972 and hindered him in 1973.

Mike Current, a pass blocker and punter at Ohio State University, spent some time on Denver and Miami taxi squads before becoming a Bronco regular. "We have a fine football team with the best coaching staff in football," Current commented in 1970. "If we do not have a winning season it would not be due to any coaching failure, but because we, as players, did not give what was needed to win."

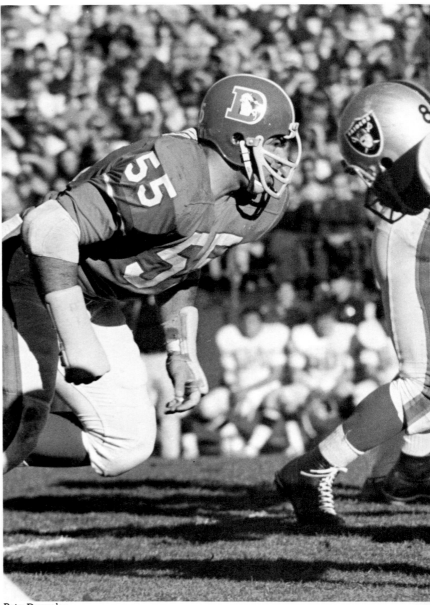

Pete Duranko

George Goeddeke

Mike Current

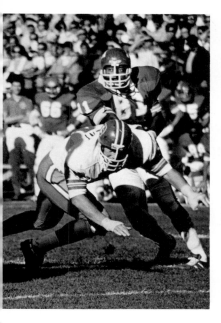

The last two nuggets of Saban's 1967 bonanza were Fran Lynch and Floyd Little. Lynch, who set rushing records at Hofstra, had his best day as a Bronco in 1968 when he scored two touchdowns in a 21-13 win over the Jets. "Fran looks frail," a teammate said, "but he is probably one of the strongest men on the Broncos. He is a hard worker and a team man above all." Fran has scored 10 touchdowns as a relief running back.

Fran Lynch

And Floyd Little . . .

A shy, silent six-year old when his father died of cancer, Floyd relied heavily on his five brothers and sisters to help him through childhood.

The Littles moved to New Haven when Floyd was 13. He later attended Bordentown Military Institute where he scored 33 touchdowns in his first football career.

More than 40 colleges bid for Little's services but Floyd selected Syracuse because they offered him an academic scholarship. "I wanted to get an education," Floyd explained, "whether I played football or not."

Saturday Evening Post writer Myron Cope asked the three-time All-American how he prepared for a game. "I drink half a glass of fresh blood on Saturday morning," Little chided Cope. "I sleep in a darkened cage and eat raw hamburger. On Saturday afternoon they let me out and I'm so happy to see light, I just run all over the place."

Cope's article included an excerpt from a paper Floyd wrote for an English composition class. "It was a lovely summer afternoon, as the waves rode the shore, bringing in the sweet smell of the ocean. While lying on the beach in deep contemplation, I watched a dog prowl slowly by. He appeared to be lost..."

"Floyd Little," wrote Larry Csonka in *Always On The Run*, "made me realize never to let the outside activities at college bother me. He wanted to play good football and get in the pros. That was his life. I made it my life too."

When he did make the pros, "he ran over his own blockers," said Fred Gehrke. "He had to learn to wait for the pulling guards."

"Floyd could not block, catch a pass, or protect himself when he got here," Gehrke continued.

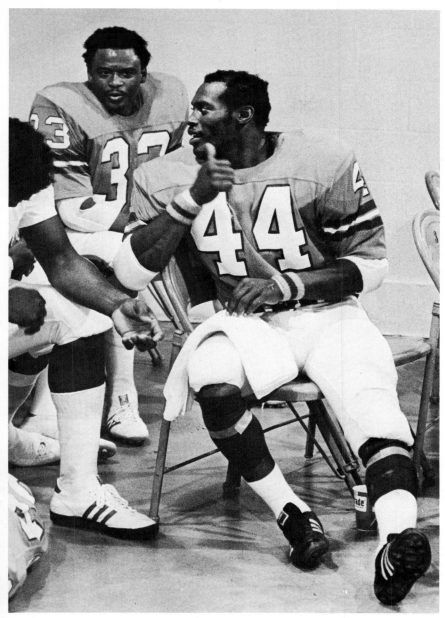

Floyd Little is active in several charitable organizations: the United Negro College Fund, UMCA, Epilepsy Foundation, March of Dimes and the NFL Drug Abuse Program. He toured Vietnam with other NFL veterans in 1970; won the Brian Piccolo Award in 1973 and the Byron White Award in 1974.

"He has a great basic philosophy towards his approach to life and to football," John Ralston told *Colorado Athlete* interviewer Mike Wolfe. "The idea is to put everything into it because you never know if it is the last time you are going to do it. If we did everything that way as individuals, I'm sure we would put just that much more into it. He is a great leader with a great basic philosophy, always gives 110 percent of himself."

"He is a great believer in self-talk," explained Ralston. "It is the idea of all our thought processes governing what we will ultimately do. He gives himself a pep talk every time he carries the football, and I like the idea. If all our guys would say to themselves, 'I have to make this the best block I have ever made' we are going to have some great plays and some great games in the future..."

"He was hampered by nagging injuries—results of the beatings he took—and still takes—in every game."

Little's pro statistics are staggering. In 1971 he led the NFL with 1,133 yards rushing. In his career Floyd has rushed, caught passes, returned punts and kickoffs for more than 10,000 yards and 49 touchdowns in seven seasons. His accomplishments off the field can never be documented.

Despite a 3-11 record, 1967 was the Broncos' first winning season. Floyd Little came to Denver.

103

From 1968 to 1971 Lou Saban's Broncos acquired offensive linemen Marv Montgomery, Larron Jackson, Mike Schnitker, Tom Lyons; receivers Mike Haffner, Bill Van Heusen, Bill Masters, Jerry Simmons; running backs Bob Anderson, Joe Dawkins; defensive linemen Paul Smith, Lyle Alzado; defensive backs Fred Forsberg, Charles Greer, Ken Criter, Bill Thompson; Randy Montgomery; Leroy Mitchell; placekickers Bobby Howfield and Jim Turner.

Little Bobby Howfield was the Bronco booter for three seasons. Denver traded the

Bobby Howfield

English soccer star to the Jets in 1971 and the following year Bobby led the AFL in scoring.

The Broncos received ex-Utah State quarterback Jim Turner in exchange for Howfield. Nicknamed "Tank" at New York, Turner tried out for the Jets after a New York at Oakland game in 1963. The Jets signed Jim in 1964 and he led the AFL in scoring in 1968-69. In 1973 Turner threw an 80-yard touchdown pass for his old college coach, John Ralston. Unfortunately Turner's toss was to an opposing lineman, San Diego's Coy Bacon.

Jim Turner

Charles Greer (20) from the University of Colorado is a steady, underrated safety. He started 55 of 56 games in a four-year span (1969-72).

The Broncos signed some great defensive backs during the Saban years.

Fred Forsberg (52) was All-Pacific Coast and Lineman of the Year at the University of Washington. Forsberg played two years with the Calgary Stampeders before signing with Denver in 1968.

Ken Criter (53) was All-Big Ten at the University of Wisconsin where he set a school record for most tackles in a season. Criter's hustle and aggressiveness on Bronco special teams resulted in the formation of the "Criter's Critters" fan club in 1973.

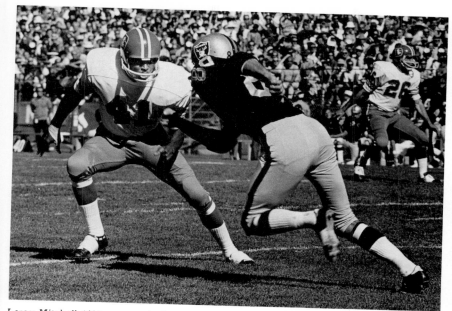

Leroy Mitchell (41) was acquired from Houston in 1971. Leroy was voted Boston's Most Valuable Player in 1968, then suffered a broken neck in 1969 training camp.

Randy Montgomery (21), from Weber State, is an art major with several local exhibitions to his credit.

Maryland State University star Bill Thompson (36) led the AFL in punt return yardage in 1969 —the only rookie ever to do so.

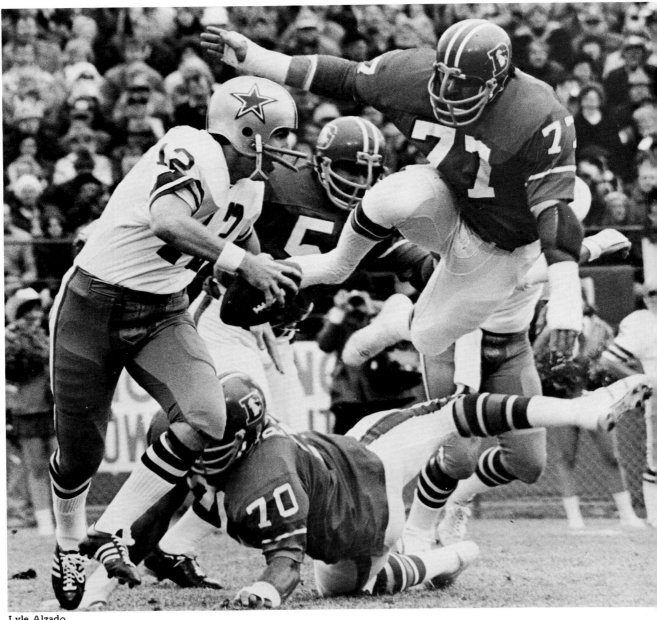

Lyle Alzado

"the desire to be the best—that's what keeps me going . . ."

Football historians claim the *blitz* was born on December 1, 1957, when the San Francisco 49ers used the new defensive weapon against the New York Giants. New York's offensive coach, Vince Lombardi, commented angrily after the game, "the blitz is used only to cover a weakness."

AFL defenses combined the blitz with the bump-and-run to make life miserable for quarterbacks. The Broncos were among the best in the business of sacking enemy passers. This tradition was perpetuated when Lou Saban added Lyle Alzado and Paul Smith to an already strong defensive line.

Alzado, Yankton College's first player to make the pros, told *Sportscope* why he selected a small school. "I'm very sensitive. I didn't want to get lost at a big university."

Sensitive Lyle is also quick and strong. The former Golden Gloves regional heavyweight champion can bench press 500 pounds. He has set Bronco hamburger-eating records; helps at his mother's flower shop; and uses his special education degree to work with Denver's disadvantaged children in the off season. "The people of Denver have been good to me," said the big bachelor, "and I want to give them something in return."

Paul Smith," states Lyle Alzado, "is the best there is. He plays 150 percent. After a game, if we lose, Paul has tears in his eyes. For a big man like that to cry, you know losing hurts."

"The *still improving* Paul Smith," claims Fred Gehrke, "has exceptional quickness in his five-yard area. He learned a lot from Rich Jackson."

He sure did. Jackson left prior to the 1972 season during which Smith racked up 47 tackles, 43 assists, 41 harassments and 11 sacks.

In 1970 the Broncos signed Colorado University All-American Bobby Anderson. As a Buffalo quarterback and halfback Anderson set 18 CU records, including rushing for 354 yards in a Liberty Bowl victory over Alabama.

Popular Bobby Anderson became the second first-round draft choice to ever sign with the Broncos in 1970.

Chronically underrated until recently, proud Paul Smith takes everything in stride—"It doesn't bother me that some of the other guys get the publicity."

Jerry Simmons

Joe Dawkins

A year after Anderson joined the team, University of Wisconsin star Joe Dawkins was acquired from Houston. Dawkins' first start at fullback followed an Anderson injury in 1972. With Little, Lynch, Anderson and Dawkins, Saban's Broncos boasted one of the best young backfields in football.

Lou also recruited and signed some talented receivers. In 1968 the Broncos obtained sure-handed Mike Haffner and a punter, halfback, quarterback, safety, flanker and scratch golfer from Maryland—Bill Van Heusen. In 1970 Denver added ex-LSU and Buffalo Bill receiver Billy Masters. In 1971 Bethune-Cookman's Jerry Simmons became a Bronco.

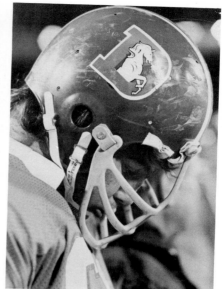

Mike Schnitker

Saban's long list of outstanding signees ended with four offensive linemen. This quartet led Denver to a new team pass-protection record in 1971.

Lakewood High School and Colorado University grad Mike Schnitker was drafted in 1969 as a defensive player. Mike made the transition to starting offensive guard, but was sidelined by an ankle injury in 1971.

Bill Van Heusen (42) leads the Broncos with seven knee operations.

(far left) Mike Haffner (84) gained fame for his diving, last-minute, game-saving catches. The former UCLA single-wing tailback and quarterback was dubbed Denver's "Super Sub" in 1968, when he played three offensive positions and held for placekicks. Mike scored seven touchdowns for the Broncos and retired in 1971.

Tom Lyons (61) is small, quick and strong. The one-time Denver Symphony Orchestra guest director told *Empire*, "I'll quit football after we reach the Super Bowl."

Marv Montgomery (78), from USC, was Denver's #1 draft pick in 1971. He broke his leg in the Broncos' 1973 victory over Pittsburgh.

Lou Saban spent almost five years as Denver's head coach and general manager. He put Alzado, Anderson, Costa, Criter Current, Dawkins, Duranko, Forsberg, Goeddeke, Greer, Haffner, L. Jackson, R. Jackson Little, Lynch, Lyons, Masters, Mitchell, M. Montgomery, R. Montgomery, Myrtle, Schnitker Simmons, Smith, Thompson, Turner, Van Heusen, and a hundred other men in Bronco uniforms. But he could never put together a winning season. Was it the way he coached? Th injuries? The trades? Denver's lack of depth? Probably a combination of all four plus th often overlooked fact that Denver was in pro football's toughest division. Lou Saban's teams were 3-24 against their AFL/AFC Western opponents— Oakland, Kansas City and San Diego. The Broncos were only two losses below .500 against the rest of the league.

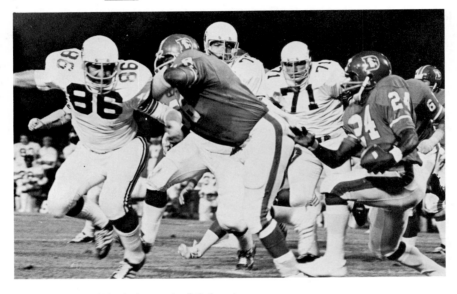

Larron Jackson (68) leads the way for Otis Armstrong.

Jerry Smith replaced Lou Saban for Denver's last five games in 1971.

hn Ralston inherited a young, rong, sound football team. alston made some coaching d personnel changes—adding a mbination of rookies and terans evenly distributed tween offense and defense. It as a winning combination.

Old leather-wise, John acquired a center, three receivers and four defensive backs. The Broncos claimed and traded for Baylor's Bobby Maples (Steelers); San Diego State's Haven Moses (Bills); Michigan State's Gene Washington (Vikings); USC's Rod Sherman (Raiders); Oregon State's Steve Preece (Eagles); Stanford's Don Parish (Cardinals); Michigan's Bill Laskey (Colts); and USC's Ray May (Colts).

While insuring stability and experience with seasoned veterans, Ralston did not forfeit Denver's future chances. He hired a whole stable of potential superstars.

Rod Sherman, a quarterback and sprinter in high school, was the Broncos' leading receiver in 1972. He caught 38 passes for 661 yards and three TDs.

y May (56) introduced "hand-holding" the defensive huddle to inspire team ity. Ray spends his spare time working h underprivileged boys.

Gene Washington, an NCAA hurdling champion, came to Denver from Minnesota in a trade for Rod Sherman.

Haven Moses (25) was unanimous Little All-American in college and was Buffalo's first draft choice in 1967.

Bobby Maples (50) was an All-Southwest Conference quarterback as a freshman. He switched to linebacker as a sophomore. Now a center, Bobby is among the best in the NFL on snapping for placekicks and punts.

Bill Laskey (45) was an All-Big Ten defensive end at the University of Michigan.

Tom Graham chats with John Ralston. Graham is very aggressive on the field. Off the field Tom uses his sociology degree to work in a juvenile rehabilitation program.

Denver's first draft choice in 1972 was big, bad Riley Odoms. The All-American rookie from the University of Houston caught 21 passes for 320 yards and one score while sharing the tight end spot with Billy Masters.

An honorable-mention All-American from the University of Oregon, Tom Graham led the Broncos with 60 tackles and 31 assists in 1972. Denver also obtained free agent Mike Simone— a standout for John Ralston at Stanford—as another linebacker.

Riley Odoms

The Broncos' first draft choice in 1973 was Otis Armstrong.

"Otis Armstrong," said Fred Gehrke, "Is probably the quickest running back I've ever seen in pro football. Otis is strong and durable. He never gets hurt. He's developing into a great receiver. And the best part is he's still young. Someday Armstrong will top his 1974 performance."

In 1974 all Armstrong accomplished was 1,407 yards rushing—best in the NFL and a Bronco season record. Otis also caught 38 passes for 405 yards and returned 16 kickoffs for 386 yards. He led Denver in scoring with 12 touchdowns for 72 points.

And he's still improving. . .

Otis Armstrong

115

John Ralston said in 1974, "I'd rather have Tom Jackson (57) than any other linebacker in football."

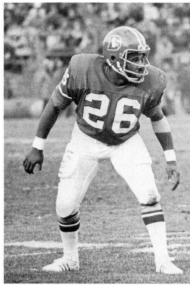

"Little" Calvin Jones (26) was one of tw[o] Bronco rookies to play every 1973 game[;] the other was Barney Chavous. Calvin in[ter]cepted four passes during the season and [was] named to the Pro Football Weekly All-Rookie team.

On defense Denver drafted South Carolina State All-American Barney Chavous; Louisville All-Missouri Valley linebacker Tom Jackson; University of Washington All-American Calvin Jones; and the Broncos obtained second-year man Maurice Tyler from Buffalo.

Barney Chavous (79) meets Dallas quarte[r]back Roger Staubach.

Maurice Tyler (23) played defensive end[,] safety, lacrosse and basketball at two dif[fer]ent colleges—Baltimore Community and Morgan State.

andy Gradishar

Claudie Minor talking with Offensive Line Coach Jerry Frei.

on Keyworth

n 1974 the Broncos added a trio
f talented rookies—Randy
radishar, Claudie Minor and
on Keyworth.

hio State coach called
radishar, "the best linebacker
e've ever had."

He's smart," added Fred Gehrke.
He plays the pass very well
ecause he's so intelligent. He
ained a lot of confidence during
is rookie year—ours and his own."

"Claudie Minor," continued
Gehrke, "Was thrown to the
wolves early. He started all 14
games for us and went up against
the NFL's best people in our first
few games. He made some
mistakes, but grew stronger each
week. He has the potential to be
an All-Pro."

"We were forced to bring Claudie
along faster than usual for a
rookie," said Jerry Frei. "But he
progressed beautifully. He has
great physical quickness and
unlimited potential."

Jon Keyworth, obtained in a trade
with Washington, amassed more
than 550 yards rushing, receiving
passes and returning kickoffs. His
ten touchdowns rushing led the
Broncos in 1974.

"Keyworth matured quickly,"
said Gehrke. "He had a little
self-confidence problem because
he played so many positions in
college. Once he settled in at
running back, he came on strong.
He will get bigger and continue
to improve."

"All these guys—Gradishar, Minor
and Keyworth—are all a full year
ahead of themselves," concluded
Gehrke. "They really saw a lot of
game time for rookies. They all
adjusted to and beat the pressure
of playing in the NFL. We expect
great things from each of them."

In the first five rounds of the 1975 draft Denver acquired eight high-quality athletes. The Broncos' first choice, and the first defensive back selected, was Louis Wright.

"He's big, fast and smooth," said Fred Gehrke. "He doesn't have much college experience behind him so we feel he's just coming into his own. He's very coachable and should make the starting team in a minimum time."

The Broncos' second selection was defensive end Charlie Smith. One of 13 children, Smith is deceptively quick. Denver coaches feel he needs more weight for his 6' 5" frame, and that the extra pounds will give him more strength.

In the third round Denver picked quarterback, fullback, punter and placekicker Mike Franckowiak and linebacker Drew Mahalic. Franckowiak has an extremely strong arm and could help the kicking teams. Mahalic's play in the 1975 Orange Bowl helped the Irish upset Alabama.

Louis Wright—San Jose State

Charlie Smith—North Carolina Central

Mike Franckowiak—Central Michigan

Drew Mahalic—Notre Dame

Steve Taylor—Georgia

Rich Upchurch—Minnesota

Rubin Carter—Miami

With four more picks in the next two rounds, Denver drafted defensive back Steve Taylor, wide receiver Rich Upchurch, offensive tackle Stan Rogers and defensive tackle Rubin Carter.

The Broncos also obtained wide receiver Jack Dolbin from the World Football League and traded Larron Jackson to Atlanta for defensive tackle Greg Marx; Bill Laskey to Detroit for guard Chuck Walton; and Lonnie Hepburn to Cleveland for linebacker Bill Andrews

"They're all great prospects," said Fred Gehrke. "Wright, Smith, Mahalic, Taylor, Carter, Marx, Andrews—they've got to help improve our defense. Upchurch and Dolbin add to an already strong, young receiving corps."

"Charley Johnson feels better than he has in years. Paul Smith and Bobby Anderson are recovering from their injuries and are actually ahead of our medical schedule for them. I'm looking forward to 1975."

Jack Dolbin—Chicago Fire

Bill Andrews—Browns

So is John Ralston. "We learned a lot about ourselves last year, both as coaches and as players," says Ralston in Denver's 1975 press guide. "We were coming off our first winning season and a near miss for a playoff berth. We were a little complacent. . . We did manage another winning season, but that's not enough anymore.

"We also learned about playing under the pressures of a contending team. We didn't sneak up on anyone in 1974, after our good season the year before. Everyone was pointing for us, and, hopefully, we learned the poise a championship team needs to go through a long season.

"We will profit from our mistakes and we will be better in 1975. . . There aren't nearly the weak spots to fill that we had three years ago. What we need most of all is a good camp so we can get all of the experimentation out of the way early and be ready to get after people on opening day, something we didn't do last year. This should be our best football team, and our squad is eager to get the 1975 season underway."

FIFTEEN MINUTES EVERY SUNDAY

Stop-watch watchers claim today's three-hour football games contain only 15 minutes of action. Those 15 minutes include about 60 running plays, some 40 passes, 30 or punts, placekicks, interceptions, touchdowns, injuries, sacks, penalties, fumbles and fans. Highlighted here, without words or further explanation, are Bronco sacks —the flip side of our quarterback record. While the offense frequently switched signal callers, Denver's defense constantly applied pressure to opposing passers. And Bronco bles—dreaded overs that win or all games. nally, Bronco eir support, and defeat, ible for ing a

ootball

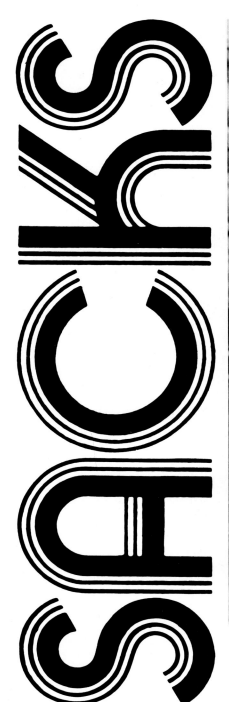

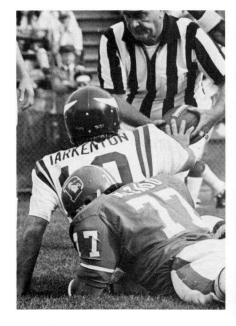

126

128

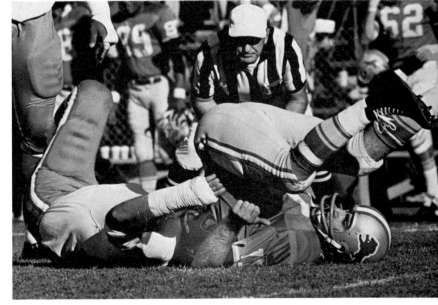

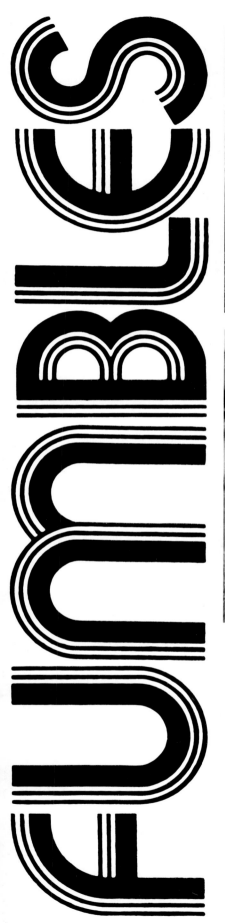

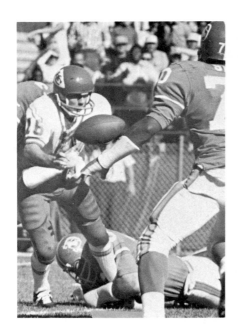

THE RALSTON YEARS

Very few National Football League teams have not made post-season appearances. In the NFC, expansion franchises Atlanta and New Orleans come up consistently empty handed. In the AFC, only Denver has never earned playoff payoffs. If anyone can take the Broncos to pro football's promised land, it will be John Ralston. Ralston spent the 1972 season learning the subtle differences between college and pro coaching. In 1973 he brought the Broncos to unknown and unexpected heights. The 1974 season, filled with injuries, tough opponents, inconsistent and erractic play, was disappointing for the Broncos and their fans. But it is John Ralston's goal that Denver "will go to and win the Super Bowl." And John Ralston does not quit until he reaches his goal . . .

1972

"Better seasons," warned Denver Post columnist Jim Graham, "Assuming intelligent and fortunate drafts, lie ahead. This Bronco team will still be fun to watch, especially as it matures over the long season. However, and this is just one man's opinion, I can't see the record being better than 4-10."

The prediction was one game short. Denver battled and bumbled to a 5-9 season. Ralston assumed personal responsibility for many of the losses. "We weren't mentally prepared," he admitted often, "And that's my fault." Graham was right about one thing. The Broncos were fun to watch.

First place in the AFC West! That's the way it was after Denver beat Houston on opening day. Oakland, Kansas City and San Diego all lost. Steve Ramsey's offense rolled up 478 yards in the 30-17 victory. During the next four weeks the Broncos caught a fast elevator to the division cellar.

It took Denver 15 seconds to score on San Diego. Randy Montgomery raced 94 yards with the opening kickoff. The Chargers dominated the next 59:45 of the game. Their defense recorded one blocked punt, five sacks and six interceptions—three each off Ramsey and Charley Johnson. Their offense posted three touchdowns in the second quarter.

"I don't know why we weren't ready," Ralston said after the 37-14 loss. "I feel a certain sense of responsibility. We were just as flat as we could be at the start. That's mental and that part is my responsibility. In that respect we weren't ready to play."

The following week Kansas City scored three last-period touchdowns to defeat Denver 45-24. Steve Ramsey lost one fumble, threw three interceptions, suffered eight sacks and had several catchable passes dropped.

"I really figured we would win today," commented Ralston. "The squad was mentally sharp and we went out and took it to them."

Denver lost their third straight game to Cincinnati. "We've started four regular season games now and scored early," explained Ralston. "Against Houston we were in deep and tried that fourth down that missed but we scored the next time we got it. Against San Diego we scored on the opening kickoff. Against Kansas City we scored on our first play. Today we get the ball on a fumble, take it right in and go up 7-0."

Seven was hardly enough. Bengal back Tommy Casanova set up one touchdown and scored another on punt returns. Ramsey went down six times in the 21-10 loss, bringing the Bronco non-protection record to 23 sacks for the season.

The next week Denver lost a "heart-breaker" to Minnesota. Floyd Little scored his third touchdown of the day to put the Broncos ahead 20-16 with 53 seconds remaining. Thirty seconds later Fran Tarkenton passed to Gene Washington for the game-winning touchdown.

"I don't think today's loss will destroy us," John Ralston whispered after the game. "You still play each game individually. If we're going to let this one upset us it will be a long year. We'll play them one by one. I can see a lot of good things here, and when it finally comes together like it did today, we'll start winning."

Cleveland came from behind to beat the Broncos 27-20. Mike Phipps celebrated Floyd Little Day at Mile High Stadium. The young quarterback threw two touchdown passes and ran for another to break a 20-20 tie.

"We had our opportunities," said Ralston. "We just didn't make them pay off. I thought when we were ahead 17-13 if we could generate some offense it might have helped us."

With the exception of Floyd Little's 55-yard touchdown run, the Broncos were unable to generate any offense against New York the following week. The Giants kept steady pressure on Charley Johnson and second-half replacement Steve Ramsey. The 29-17 loss gave Denver a dismal 2-5 record midway through the '72 campaign.

Ralston was obviously displeased. "We didn't sack their quarterback. We didn't tackle. We didn't play the ball well in the air. And our offense didn't get in when we had opportunities."

The unpredictable Broncos followed their East Coast loss with a 16-10 win in Los Angeles. Trailing 10-7, Jim Turner kicked three fourth-quarter field goals while Denver's defense shut out the Rams. Ralston teams seem to shine in West Coast games. After the victory the freshman coach was awarded his first pro game ball.

Seeking their second straight upset win, Denver took a 10-7 first-quarter lead over Oakland. Then, in Ralston's words, "They just beat the devil out of us."

Charley Johnson's two TD passes were no match for Oakland's incredible offensive display. The Raiders scored on seven of their 10 possessions, played the entire game without punting, and eventually won easily 37-20.

Denver's four-game losing streak ended abruptly at Oakland. Charley Johnson, in his first Bronco start, completed 20 of 28 passes for 361 yards and two touchdowns to beat the Raiders 30-23. The offensive line surrendered no sacks for the second straight week.

With team morale waning and fan pressure building, it was a much needed victory. Floyd Little said, "It was the biggest win since I've been a Bronco."

Jim Graham wrote, "Ralston's positive thinking approach is starting to pay big dividends. These young Broncos sincerely believe in it and more importantly in themselves."

Denver needed to sweep their final four games to salvage a break-even, 7-7, season. The Broncos played well enough to win the last four, but they had to settle with a 2-2 split.

Atlanta, completely dominated by Denver all day, somehow won the game 23-20. "They took advantage of every break they got," explained Ralston.

Then Kansas City, with absolutely no offense, beat the Broncos 24-21. Charley Johnson threw two interceptions for touchdowns and fumbled to set up another Chief score.

"Three mistakes—21 points," said Charley. "We played so well otherwise it kills me to be the one that kept us from winning. It should have been a shutout. The defense played extremely well. We moved the ball, then made key mistakes."

The Broncos rebounded with two impressive wins. Denver beat San Diego 38-13 on two TD receptions by Haven Moses, a 65-yard scoring punt return by Charles Greer, and touchdowns by Floyd Little and Joe Dawkins.

"Winning games," said Ralston, "is the most important thing for Denver at this stage. This is only the second time in 12 years the Broncos won their next-to-last game."

It became the first time Denver ever won their last two games when the Broncos beat New England 45-21. Floyd Little's two touchdowns gave him a team record 13 for the season. Haven Moses scored twice; Fran Lynch and Rod Sherman also scored TDs in the Bronco rout.

Ralston, looking back over the season, commented, "We could have had a winning season if we'd won the close ones."

And Jim Graham summarized 1972 optimistically. "The Broncos are not that far from getting over the hump."

For 13 glorious weeks the Bronco Express rolled along, sputtering at first, then gathering speed and momentum, and finally pulling into the last station at Oakland with everything on the line. It was just not to be. An up-tight first half, Charley's concussion, the controversial fake punt, and Denver's season was over. The Mighty Ralston Players fell a few points short of winning the AFC West. Another break during the season—one less penalty, one more field goal, even a clean snap on the fake punt might have meant the championship. Here are excerpts from articles written by sportswriters assigned to Bronco opponents in 1973—Denver's first winning season in history.

NIGHTMARE IN DENVER

by Dick Forbes,
Cincinnati Enquirer   Sept. 17

Three long, well-executed scoring drives in the first half, and another late in the game when ball possession was paramount, sent Cincinnati's proud defensive corps reeling here Sunday.

The utter breakdown of the defense against quarterback Charley Johnson, running back Floyd Little, plus inability of Bengal receivers to catch passes that were laid in their hands, helped make it easy for the Denver Broncos to rip Cincinnati 28-10 before 49,059 on the soggy, slippery turf of Mile High Stadium.

The aroused Broncos, showing the smooth coaching touch of John Ralston, wrecked completely the Bengal's hopes for getting off to a fast start in the new National Football League season.

Bengal quarterback Ken Anderson said after the game he wouldn't let the defeat disturb him and praised the Broncos, "They're going to give a lot of people a lot of trouble this year."

GOSSETT SAVES 49ERS

by Darrell Wilson,
San Francisco Chronicle Sept. 24

With 26 seconds left in an ebb-and-flow game in which the scoring spurts by each team were inspired by the emotional impact of one or two big plays, this one was Bruce Gossett's to win or lose.

Gossett lined up at the 39, a strong wind in his face, and kicked the field goal that gave the 49ers a 36-34 victory over Denver. It was Bruce's fifth, without a miss, thereby setting a 49er team record and a personal one for him.

The 49ers, unable to do anything right for the first 13 minutes, and trailing 13-0, had gained inspiration on one big play, a 48-yard pass from John Brodie to Jim Thomas. That led immediately to a 22-yard fielder by Gossett, who also was to kick them from 14, 39 and 46 yards before his game-winner.

There were 50,996 rabid Bronco fans on hand and those sitting directly above the press box nearly stomped their way through the roof while Denver was rallying from a 30-13 deficit to the 34-33 lead.

San Francisco coach Dick Nolan said, "Denver has a fine offensive team, which we knew, but we had five interceptions and we should never have let ourselves get into the position of having to win it with a field goal."

Denver coach John Ralston said, "We didn't save anything, we used it all. I was very pleased with the way our team came back. I've been watching John Brodie play for almost 20 years and I thought today's performance was one of his best under pressure."

DENVER'S "DIRTY TRICKS" BACKFIRE

by Don Pierson,
Chicago Tribune Press Service

The Denver Broncos tried to out-muscle, out-talk, and out-penalty the Chicago Bears, and failed on all three counts.

They were no match for the bruising style of football Abe Gibron loves, and they fumbled and bumbled their way to a 33-14 defeat in which Bronco after Bronco was helped off the field.

By the time the incredibly long affair was half over, Gibron was yelling at the 51,159 fans in Mile High Stadium who had been yelling at him earlier. And Denver coach John Ralston admitted his team played "pretty lousy" football.

"They were wild," said tackle Randy Jackson. "They have always been physical, but they were playing wild football, and it hurt them."

"They tried to play like the Bears," said safety Garry Lyle. "And they ended up taking cheap shots."

"They've been holding on defense for three weeks and getting away with it," said Dick Butkus. "Paul Brown filed a complaint to the league office. We saw it in the films. On the bump-and-run, you usually end up holding, and today it caught up with them."

"They helped us with all those quotes before the game, too," said Gibron, "and that TV show before the game."

Denver's Haven Moses had said he thought the Bronco receivers could beat the Bear defenders and the Bronco line could protect Charley Johnson.

"Maybe we shouldn't have said anything," said Ralston.

With the score 30-0, Gibron was yelling at Moses, "Hey, movie star, how do you like this?"

Denver errors cost them the game. In the first three quarters the Bears got 16 breaks, including three fumbles by Floyd Little, two interceptions, and enough penalties to cause fans to nearly attack the officials on their way to the dressing room. They flagged the Broncos eight times for 62 costly yards, but the Bears, who refused to be out-hit or out-talked, even won the penalty game with 12 for 132 yards.

CHIEFS STYMIE BRONCOS

by Bill Richardson,
Kansas City Times   *Oct. 8*

Playing King of the Mountain was a game-long struggle for the Chiefs yesterday as they fought off the Denver Broncos, 16-14, and held top spot in the AFC West.

In fact, the Chiefs fought an uphill battle before finally gaining the upper hand on Jan Stenerud's 39-yard field goal with less than seven minutes to play. Then came the perilous task of defending the lead as the touchdown-underdog Broncos got two more shots at their first victory ever in Kansas City. But they didn't pull it off, failing for the 11th straight time here.

Part of the Broncos' failure in the clutch could be attributed to questionable offensive strategy in the final two minutes. Facing a third-and-two on the Denver 31, Charley Johnson chose a sideline pass to Riley Odoms. With the receiver squeezed in at the sidelines, Johnson overthrew. On fourth down the Broncos tried the running play and Buck Buchanan and Willie Lanier stopped Floyd Little for only a yard. Three Chief plays later the game was over. You have to wonder if the Broncos couldn't have gained the first down on two rushes.

Floyd Little, a gifted runner, threaded the sidelines for a 50-yard touchdown on a short pass from Johnson in the second quarter. In the fourth quarter Johnson caught the Chiefs in a zone and sent Joe Dawkins through the line on what the coaches call a sucker play for a 72-yard touchdown. That run put the Broncos on top with 10 minutes left. The Chiefs came back on a drive from their own 10 to set up Stenerud's 39-yard winner. Kansas City spent the rest of the afternoon tenaciously guarding first place.

BRONCS BASH OILERS

by David Casstevens,
Houston Post

Charley Johnson, the guy who once wore a Columbia blue hospital gown, proved again he's the biggest item to hit Denver since snow tires.

Facing a patchwork man-for-man secondary, the Broncos' aging but accurate quarterback threw for four touchdowns, broke the 20,000 yard career passing mark and sent the winless Houston Oilers to their 16th consecutive defeat, 48-20.

Whoever called him Sweet Charley anyway?

In two years as an Oiler, the 34-year-old veteran had surgery no less than five times, but on this storybook Sunday Johnson wielded the scalpel on the very team that sent him to the Rockies' rarified air for a third round draft choice last season.

Johnson hit Haven Moses with touchdown passes of 19, 33 and three yards. Then in the fourth period, after at least half the Astrodome's 32,801 witnesses had already departed, Mr. Scar Tissue connected on a 62-yard score to a young man who sounds more like a dress shirt than a wide receiver, Bill Van Heusen.

"They came out in a man-for-man all day long and I was really surprised. It was a sign of complete disregard for my passing ability," Johnson explained later. "You know, I hadn't seen that much man-for-man since the mid-Sixties."

Operating from a shallow but sturdy pocket, Johnson made his task look about as difficult as dynamiting little fish. He picked apart the corners, manned by Willie Alexander and Benny

Johnson, and when both starters were temporarily withheld because of injuries, he burned all the Oilers had in reserve.

When Johnson wasn't passing for his 214 yards, he was slipping the ball to Floyd Little. Denver's record running back occasionally pierced the middle of the Oiler line, but usually skirted the flanks to keep scoring drives alive. Little carried 19 times for 123 yards and scored from four yards after a Ken Burrough fumble, one of four the Oilers lost to the Broncos.

Add a 32-yard Jim Turner field goal and Bill Thompson's 59-yard interception return and Denver had more than enough points to offset an Oiler team that played well enough to win—for a half.

Believe it or not, at one time the Oilers led, 20-10.

Skip Butler hit field goals of 20 and 49 yards, Fred Willis punctuated a 41-yard scoring drive with a burst from four yards and Burrough scored from 19 yards out on an end-around.

With four minutes left in the half, Johnson retaliated with his 33-yarder to Moses, who streaked down the sideline, slipped behind Zeke Moore and Alexander and pulled the ball into his chest as he back-peddled into the end zone.

Four plays later Dan Pastorini almost lost his life. Ray May, the Baltimore ex, ambushed the Oiler quarterback from the blind side. Pastorini hit the floor like he'd been blackjacked and the ball popped free at the Oiler 37. Six plays later Johnson flipped a three-yarder to Moses, putting Denver ahead to stay.

Throughout the one-sided second half, it seemed as if all the Broncos' front four—Barney Chavous, Paul Smith, Lyle Alzado and Pete Duranko—were part of the Oilers' offensive backfield. They wrestled Pastorini. Alzado once grabbed his white jersey and spun him around like a square dancer. Even though Pastorini was sacked three times, Alzado insisted Dante was a friend.

"We were roommates at an all-star game," Alzado said. "Really, we're good friends. I talked to Dan a little during the game. I told him, 'Dan, I'm coming' again and again.'"

The verdict was secure when Lynn Dickey entered the game but the Broncos' treatment didn't change. They sacked Dickey four times and forced Pastorini's backup to fumble at the Oiler seven, a mistake that set up Turner's 12-yard field goal to end the scoring.

While Alvin Haymond didn't score, the Oiler return specialist was Houston's most explosive weapon during the long afternoon. The Washington Redskin ex, activated this week, returned three kickoffs for 81 yards and traveled another 73 yards with three Van Heusen punts.

Haymond's 44-yard punt return in the third period gave the Oilers possession at the Denver 47, but on the first play Burrough fumbled a screen pass and the Broncos recovered.

At that point, the Astrodome began to empty.

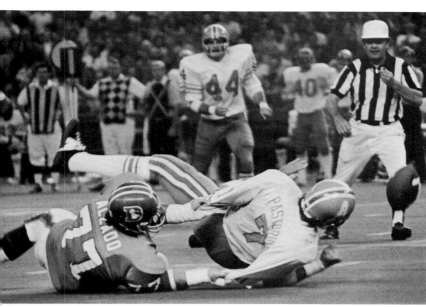

All hopes that the Oilers might rally extinguished early in the third period when Pastorini dropped back, threw over the middle toward tight end Dave Parks and Thompson stepped in for an easy theft.

"The blitz was on," explained Pastorini.

Which linebacker blitzed? "All of them."

First place was theirs for the taking, but like almost everything else, the Oakland Raiders couldn't get a good grip on it. Instead, they had to settle for a 23-23 deadlock with the Denver Broncos and a tie with the Kansas City Chiefs for first in the AFC West.

It was a night of misfortune for Oakland, but it appeared that George Blanda salvaged it with a 49-yard field goal with 36 seconds remaining. However, the Broncos retaliated with Jim Turner's 35-yarder three seconds before the finish in the best Blanda tradition to send Denver's first-ever Monday night crowd home howling.

"It's always better to be the tie-er than the tie-ee," said tying coach John Ralston. "It was kind of fun. It's always good when you come back like that. It should help us. But a tie, even a major one, doesn't do it. It's something on the plus side and we hope it can be a springboard because we still think Oakland is the best around.

BRONCOS DOWN JETS ON FIRST-HALF SURGE

by Murray Chase,
New York Times

The Jets played what might have been the poorest half in their history as the Denver Broncos trampled them 40-28 in the Jets' home opener.

The Broncos scored three touchdowns in 96 seconds in the first quarter for a 21-0 lead. Charley Johnson passed 15 yards to Gene Washington and 21 yards to Riley Odoms for two of the touchdowns. The other was on Leroy Mitchell's 40-yard dash with a Demory interception that was tipped by Margene Adkins, the intended receiver.

While the Broncos stopped the Jets' offense, the Jets did nothing to slow down the Denver attack. "We just played a very embarrassing defensive ball game," said Charley Winner, the defensive mastermind. "We didn't do anything well. We didn't cover well and we didn't tackle well."

"We had missed tackles after missed tackles," added Winner's father-in-law, head coach Weeb Ewbank.

DENVER TD PLAN FOILED BY LATE BIG RED STAND

by Tom Barnidge,
St. Louis Post-Dispatch

It seemed to be a time for celebration. An occasion for back-slapping and hand-clapping.

How often does a football team in need of an interception get one with two minutes, 19 seconds left in the game? How often does a team in search of quick yardage travel 41 yards in three plays? How often does a team behind by three points catch up with one second showing on the clock?

But there were no backs slapped in the Denver Broncos' dressing room at Busch Stadium. There were no hands shaken after a 17-17 tie with the Cardinals.

"We didn't come here to tie," said Denver coach John Ralston. I'll tell you that. If we'd have gained any part of that yardage, we'd have gone for the touchdown."

The yardage the Broncos couldn't gain was inside the Big Red's five-yard line. After travelling 31 yards in the flick of a couple Charley Johnson passes, the Broncos were busted. Three cracks at a game-winning touchdown found the Broncos still at the five and placekicker Jim Turner trotting onto the field.

Turner's 12-yard boot was partial redemption for his three earlier misses, from 42, 44 and 45 yards out. "This is the same as a loss for us," Turner said. "Ties are for Christmas."

Each of Turner's attempts was on line, but short. Holder Charley Johnson offered an explanation, "Jimmy was trying to be a little too sure of his direction."

Johnson also had an explanation for the Broncos' inability to push across the winning touchdown. "The first play we called was a play we got a first down with earlier in a short-yardage situation," he said. Floyd Little crashed into the right side of the line. No gain.

"The second play was a trap," Johnson said. "We thought they would be overplaying the run and we could get it through." Little took off over right guard. Gain of two yards.

"The third play was a flood. Our guys in the press box thought it would work." Little was thrown for a two-yard loss.

"It was just a frustrating game," said Johnson, peeling off layers of tape, "and we couldn't get any momentum going."

One of the Bronco momentum stoppers was Bill Thompson. He snared the key interception that gave Johnson the ball and good field position as the waning moments slipped away.

"I was looking for that pattern," he said of the corner route run by the Big Red's Ahmad Rashad. "He'd run it before and we were set up. It was a well thrown ball and Rashad was there. This time, we just got lucky."

Thompson wasn't as lucky earlier in the fourth quarter. After the Broncos took a 14-10 lead, they yielded yardage grudgingly to their own 28. Then Thompson and company were zapped for a 27-yard reception by Jackie Smith.

"That one hurt us," said Thompson. "That was a big play."

Thompson almost sounded as if the Broncos had lost. And some of them apparently believed they did.

BRONCOS SPOIL BID BY WALLER

by Jerry Magee,
San Diego Union   Nov. 12

They came, so to speak, in disguise, but beneath it, under all the fancy formations and all the motion and filigree, the San Diego Chargers are still the Chargers.

They still fumble. They still lose. They lost to Denver 30-19 in a football game they had an opportunity to win but for the thing which frustrated them through Harland Svare's coaching tenure and has now carried over to Tom Waller's, turnovers.

The Chargers, in their first appearance for Waller, on a beautiful Indian summer afternoon in Colorado before a Mile High Stadium assembly of 51,706, reached a new level. They were entertaining.

Waller spotted people all over the place. He had four guys lining up in the backfield, shifts, motions, reverses, outside receivers throwing intercepted passes, everything, including the famous defensive-tackle-intercepts-pass-by-field-goal-kicker-and-runs-for-touchdown play.

The passer was Jim Turner, once a quarterback at Utah State, who should know better. The tackle was Coy Bacon, who inched 80 yards to make it 10-9, Denver, in the second period.

Charley Johnson, an old quarterback and wise, won it for the Broncos in the second half with two touchdown passes on third-and-ten situations. One went to Riley Odoms from the Charger 14; the other to Gene Washington from the San Diego 19.

A Ray Wersching field goal brought the Chargers to within four points, at 23-19, with 4:25 left on the clock. But after a costly fumble the Broncos scored again and despite the afternoon's variety, things began to look terribly familiar.

157

STEELERS CAN'T BUST BRONCOS

by Jack Sell,
Pittsburgh Post-Gazette   Nov. 19

The Steelers just can't beat the Denver Broncos.

Yesterday in Three Rivers Stadium the Rocky Mountain club made it a sweep of three meetings with the Black and Gold under guidance of three different coaches when they rallied for 10 points to break a fourth quarter 13-13 tie and take away a well-earned 23-13 victory.

A crowd of 48,580 saw coach Chuck Noll's defensive giants give up the most points of the season to the underdog invaders of coach John Ralston.

A 46-yard field goal by the veteran Jim Turner, which hit the crossbar and bounced over, plus a two-yard pass from old-timer Charley Johnson to tight end Riley Odoms in the final six minutes swayed the decision.

Coach Ralston's victors, who haven't lost in the last six weeks, kept their title hopes alive in the Western Division. Ralston, thinking about the post-season playoffs and a possible Steeler-Bronco rematch, said, "They'll be a different club next time we play them."

The locals had their chances and had no one to blame but themselves for the loss. They fumbled three times and lost the trio, two of them on kickoffs which led to a Denver touchdown and field goal.

Johnson committed two fumbles and Dawkins another but Charley dove on all three to avert any trouble. The game seesawed until the Broncos' final 10-point splurge.

Turner booted three fielders of 32, 11 and 46 yards, and failed on a longie of 52. Roy Gerela hit from the 15 and 13 after going wide on his first try of 23. The two gave him a career aggregate of 63, beating Lou Michaels' record of 62.

Floyd Little, the 5-10, 190-pound workhorse from Syracuse, galloped 88 yards in 27 carries. Little complimented the Pittsburgh defense after the game. "I'd quit," the veteran runner remarked, "if I had to run against the Steelers every Sunday."

Little's running mate, Joe Dawkins, added 57 yards on 13 carries. The Steelers' Franco Harris took third honors with 53 yards on 11 trips.

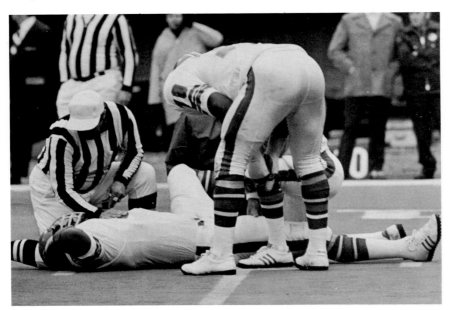

The Broncos lost left offensive tackle Marv Montgomery with 5:18 left in the first half when he suffered a broken left leg and had to be taken to the hospital in an ambulance.

Mean Joe Green, hospitalized with a strained back in mid-week, failed to start for the first time in his pro career. He did get into action with 13:04 left in the last quarter in place of Tom Keating.

he Broncos cashed in on a
umble in the first two minutes
f the game. Rocky Bleier
arried Turner's kickoff back 15
ards to his own 20 but let
oose of the ball when hit hard.
aurice Tyler grabbed it and
an five yards to the 15.

he visitors weren't warmed up
ther. Johnson fumbled but
covered for a five-yard loss.
hen L. C. Greenwood sacked
im for five more. A pass to
ene Washington sailed wide.
o Turner booted a 32-yard
elder to put the enemy in
ont 3-0.

ess Pearson started the
teelers on a promising drive
ith a 20-yard kickoff return to
s own 34. The drive sagged on
e Bronco 16. Gerela tried a
3-yard field goal, but was wide
the right.

ate in the period, the Steelers
oved to the Denver eight.
erela made it 3-3 with a
5-yarder.

the second quarter, Gerela
nt an 18-yard fielder through
e posts but Lyle Alzado was
lled for roughing the kicker.
he Steelers took the penalty,
pping for a TD, but Denver
ld and they had to settle for
15-yarder and a 6-3 lead.

he Broncos put on their best
ive of the half, moving to the
ome four. Turner's 11-yarder
ade it 6-6 at halftime.

The winners dominated the
third quarter in which they
scored the go-ahead touchdown
and held the home club without
a first down and to only six
offensive plays. Otis Armstrong
got them off flying with a
32-yard kickoff return to the
Denver 33.

The Broncos needed only 10
plays to tally a TD but the
biggest was contributed by an
official, Jimmy Cole. He called
a 25-yard pass interference
penalty against Mel Blount, who
leaped to stop a heave intended
for ex-Steeler Jerry Simmons.
That brought a first down on
the local 28. Eventually Little
drove over left tackle for the
final 10 yards. Turner converted
and the Broncs were in front
again, 13-6.

The Steelers struck back early
in the last quarter with an
80-yard advance in four plays
for the equalizer. After Bill Van
Heusen's punt into the end
zone, the locals scrimmaged at
their 20. Terry Hanratty tossed
19 yards to Frank Lewis. Harris
ran right end for four. Hanratty
found John McMakin for 15
then whipped one 43 yards to
Ron Shanklin in the left corner
of the end zone. Gerela's PAT
tied it at 13-13.

The grid fortunes now turned
their back on Rooney U.

A Bronco advance was stymied
and Turner lined up for a
46-yard field goal. It hit the
crossbar and bounced over for
three points and a 16-13 lead.

Steve Davis fumbled the next
kickoff and Tyler recovered at
the local 27. The invaders went
in for another touchdown on a
two-yard toss from Johnson to
Odoms. Turner's conversion
made it 23-13 at the final gun.

So John Ralston joins Lou
Saban and Jerry Smith as
tormentors of the Steelers.

CHIEFS' LAST GASP FALLS A BOBBLE SHORT

by Bill Richardson,
Kansas City Times   *Nov. 26*

Make no mistake about it, the
Denver Broncos are for real.
They proved it for any doubters
with a 14-10 victory over the
Kansas City Chiefs in a frantic
finish to a big game that
boosted the Broncos into first
place in the American Football
Conference West.

Long the doormat of the
division, the surging Broncos,
cheered on by an enthusiastic
crowd of 51,331, knocked the
Chiefs out of the top spot and
advanced another step toward
the first winning campaign in
their 14-year history.

With three games remaining in
the National Football League
regular season, Denver stands
6-3-2. The Chiefs dropped to
a second-place tie with Oakland
at 6-4-1.

The Chiefs didn't go down
without a fight. Snapping out of
a two-quarter slump and
fighting a 14-3 deficit, they
closed to 14-10 on an 80-yard
drive in the fourth period. Then,
racing the clock inside two
minutes, they put together
another drive to the Denver 42.

But the Kansas City first-place margin crumbled on one final salvage attempt. Mike Livingston's strike to Gary Butler at the Broncos' 24 bounced off the rookie tight end into the hands of safety Charlie Greer for a killing interception. Only 40 seconds remained, and two plays later it was over, with the exuberant Broncos making the "We're Number 1" sign on the sidelines.

The Chiefs had the momentum going at the time, and it is not inconceivable they would have marched into the end zone. Of course, the Chiefs had control of the game early too, and let it slip from their grasp. Failure to cash an interception by safety Mike Sensibaugh into any kind of points in the second quarter gave the Broncos a gigantic lift.

The Chiefs, who had taken a 3-0 lead early in the second quarter on Jan Stenerud's 15-yard field goal after a 62-yard march, got the ball on the Denver 28 after the interception. On third-and-four Will Ellison was stopped for only a two-yard gain. It looked like a 6-0 lead as Stenerud trotted on for a field-goal attempt. His kick was wide to the right.

The Broncos took new heart at shutting the Chiefs off without point and zipped to two touchdowns in the final five minutes of the half. Charley Johnson took them on an 80-yard march getting the TD on an 18-yard pitch to Haven Moses.

An interception by Calvin Jones at midfield presented Denver with another chance and Johnson siezed it. He found Moses open at the Kansas City 5 and the receiver did the rest, evading Jim Marsalis and racing goalward. Moses paid a price for the points as he was nailed by Willie Lanier at the end-zone flag.

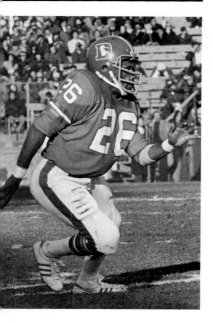

With a 14-3 lead the Broncos appeared in charge of the game. Their aroused defense, keeping pressure on Livingston, blunted Kansas City efforts in the third quarter. But Denver's offense was also slowed by the Chiefs and the 14-3 count held entering the fourth quarter.

Here the Chiefs came back for their 80-yard march, kept alive by punter Jerrel Wilson's pass to Wendell Hayes for a nine-yard gain. Livingston completed three throws in the march before hurling a pass to Otis Taylor in the back of the end zone for a seven-yard score.

After the touchdown the Chiefs forced a punt, getting the ball on their 22 with 2:08 remaining. If the Chiefs could threaten, the nationwide television audience would get a thrilling finish.

The Chiefs cooperated. After an incomplete pass Livingston zipped a 25-yarder to Otis Taylor at the Kansas City 47. Then Livingston was sacked by Paul Smith, Denver's top defensive lineman, before winging a 15-yard throw to Butler at the Bronco 44. Jeff Kinney drove for the first down at the 42 as the clock dipped under the one-minute mark.

Next was the pass that got away from Butler. But Greer, the free safety, was sure-handed and clutched the bounding ball, assuring the for-real Broncos of first place. It was only the Chiefs' third loss in history to the Broncos, all in Denver. Both Kansas City and Denver face showdown battles next Sunday. The Chiefs return home to play Cleveland while the Broncos meet Dallas in Denver.

COWBOY DEFENSE TURNS DENVER OVER

by Bob St. John,
Dallas Morning News

Dallas beat a good Denver team with another fine defensive performance. The offense, unable to mount a running game, found the knockout punch in the final period. The final score of 22-10 might not indicate it but the Cowboys had no secure feeling until a final period strike.

The game began in favorable elements but by the final period darkness had set in, the wind was gusting up to 25 miles per hour and the 50-degree temperatures seemed much colder. Snow fell later.

Roger Staubach, who hung in tough all afternoon under a heavy rush, had just hit fullback Walt Garrison for a 28-yard gain and Dallas had a first-and-ten at the Bronco 27. About the only luck the Cowboys had was on passes and bootlegs where Staubach came out of the pocket. Tom Landry, who went back to play calling for this one, picked a good number.

Staubach faked to Calvin Hill and faded back. He keyed the linebackers. If Ray May blitzed, it meant tight end Jean Fugett was probably loose coming across the middle. If not, Staubach would look for wide receiver Drew Pearson, cutting across the middle deeper than Fugett.

May was coming. Instead of dropping straight back, Staubach went to his right and quickly hit Fugett, who was all alone around the 20 and legged it on in for the touchdown. This gave Dallas a 20-3 lead 56 seconds into the final period and Landry said, "That put us in pretty good shape. Roger did a tremendous job on the play. May was right after him."

Dallas was not able to do what it felt it could do—run. The Cowboys compiled just 74 net yards rushing and a 1.9 average per attempt, a year low. But Staubach found some success on play action and the Cowboys were once again able to rely on the defense.

Denver was checked with 229 net yards and 76 of this came on a touchdown drive, terminating with less than two minutes to play, after Dallas had scored its 22nd point when Ben Barnes tackled Denver punter Bill Van Heusen in the end zone on a fake kick.

enver quarterback Charley
ohnson has seldom been
apped all season but Dallas got
him five times and defensive
ays set up the first 10
owboy points.

iddle linebacker Lee Roy
rdan stripped Joe Dawkins of
e ball and tackle Bob Lilly
cked it up and ran six yards
the Bronco five near the end
the first period. Unfortu-
tely Lilly tore a muscle above
s knee and might not be able

to play next week. Fortunately,
Staubach found Fugett for a
six-yard touchdown on second
down. Two tight ends were in
the game and Fugett was on the
right side. Staubach faked a
trap, kept and looked. Fugett
feinted a step outside and cut
back across the middle. Only
5-7 cornerback Calvin Jones
picked him up. "Roger saw the
short man and lofted the ball
over him," said Jean, who made
a fine catch.

Bill Gregory, replacing Lilly,
slapped the ball loose from
Johnson late in the second
period and end Harvey Martin
recovered at the Bronco 29 to
set up Tony Fritsch's 21-yard
field goal.

"Our defense is playing excellent," said Landry. "That's been
the difference for us and if it
keeps going, we've got a chance.
Defense is usually what it comes
down to in this league."

Denver shocked the Cowboys with its own defense, which has come on strong in the last few weeks. The Bronco front four was outstanding, and tackle Paul Smith was the best defender on the field. He had 14 tackles, nine unassisted, and two sacks, one single-handed. Dallas had studied Smith on films and found that he appeared to react a little slowly to blocks, and that other teams had been able to run by him. In this game, he was reacting better.

"Denver played exceptionally well on defense," said Landry. "I don't remember anyone shutting off our running game like that. Smith was super. He just had a super game."

"They were tough," agreed Hill who came into this game needing 67 yards to reach 1,000. "Everywhere I'd go, they were there." Hill gained just 52 yards on 22 carries, an average of only 2.7. He'll have 1,000 if he can gain 15 yards against Washington next week.

Dawkins, who committed the costly fumble, averaged 5.2 yards per carry with 12 rushes for 62 yards. He also caught five passes. Floyd Little, the all-pro, was no factor. He managed just 15 yards in nine carries, and dropped three passes in his hands.

It was not a good day to throw because of the wind. But Staubach, though sacked six times, hit 14 of 18 passes for 240 yards and two touchdowns. It was difficult to gauge Landry's play calling because there was no rushing game, the catalyst of an offense.

Johnson was good on 12 of 27 passes for 175 yards. He hit five of six for 69 yards in the TD drive, which carried 76 yards and terminated with a 17-yard TD throw to tight end Riley Odoms with 1:31 left to play. Jim Turner then hit a fine onside kick which Denver recovered but it was too late.

A large number of the 51,508 who attended in Mile High Stadium had already gone when the Broncos finally scored. The loss dropped the Broncos a half game behind Oakland in the AFC West and so the Broncos could still do it in their division. And Dallas must beat the Redskins next week to gain a playoff spot.

"BUNDLE OF MISTAKES"

Staff Special,
Dallas Morning News

"We have had to be high for two weeks in a row," coach John Ralston said between gulps of black coffee. "I guess we were due to make a bundle of mistakes."

"I just can't say enough about Roger Staubach. He is a fine quarterback who pinpointed 'em where we weren't. He was really on the stick. His accuracy was incredible the way he laid the ball in there," added Ralston, "We were probably too concerned about his ability to run and forgot that he is such a good thrower."

The Broncos, who hadn't been beaten in seven weeks (including two ties), had a total of seven penalties which helped cripple possible drives. Denver's field position was also a chilling factor on a cold, blustery, windy day.

After winning the coin toss, the Broncos elected to receive against a strong wind. "Looking back," said Ralston, "it wasn't a good day for field position and we might have made a mistake and should have kicked off."

The touchdown pass that put the game away for Dallas, Ralston felt, came with strong safety Charles Greer on the bench with a pulled hamstring. Staubach had tried the counter-flow pass early in the game and Greer had read it.

"It's a very difficult pattern for the safety to read," Ralston said. "I know Charlie knew about it, but he was injured and Maurice Tyler was in there probably looking at it for the first time."

Ralston added, "We kicked our left safety too far over (to cover the flow) and our middle line-backer was blitzing. Anyway, we didn't get the safety back there on Fugett."

The Broncos' coach had nothing but praise for Dallas but felt "we just blew it" on his return to the locker room. "They have no weaknesses and are very sound defensively. They didn't give us much in the way of holes anywhere."

As for Denver having 12 men on the field on Dallas' missed field goal in the second period, Ralston blamed his staff and himself, "It was crucial and dumb on our part, but the coaches are to blame."

"We made one adjustment this week and even that caught up with us," he said, referring to having both Tom Jackson and John Grant on the field. Tony Fritsch's field goal missed but the ensuing five-yard penalty gave Dallas a first down on the Denver 18 and Fritsch was able to later boot Dallas to a 10-0 lead.

Denver's Bill Van Heusen tried to run out of the end zone on a fourth period punt but was smothered for a safety. "We were thinking of running from the punt on the previous series," Ralston said. "We were close to midfield then and should have done it. We talked about it . . ."

Ralston had predicted that Denver would "throw a snow storm" at Dallas as part of their game plan. An hour after the game, orange-clad fans were battling a ground blizzard to get out of post-game traffic snarls.

"We thought we would throw and scratch around and see where we could run," Ralston said of his actual game plan. "But they kept changing defenses on Charley and he wasn't getting the protection he needed. Dallas is a very sound team, and like I said, they didn't give us any holes."

CHARGERS NO BRONCO BUSTERS

by Chuck Sawyer,
San Diego Union

It was a day of contrasting hopes and ambitions, and when it was over the rich had become richer and the poor got beaten.

On one hand there were the Denver Broncos, assuring themselves of their first winning season and producing a showdown battle at Oakland next weekend for the championship of the American Football Conference West.

On the other, there were the San Diego Chargers whose 42-28 loss made certain the team's worst season in history. There were 44,494 in the stands hoping for what many figured might be a small miracle on the last-chance day of the home season, a miracle that was not to be.

More than 1,000 members of the Broncos QB Club basked in warm sunshine as their team rolled up 42 points on four Jim Turner field goals, touchdown runs by Floyd Little and Joe Dawkins, touchdown receptions by Riley Odoms and Haven Moses, and a safety when Dennis Partee's punt was blocked out of the end zone.

The Bronco fans came complete with cheer leaders attired in cowgirl outfits and displayed an oversized banner which said: "When the Broncos Ride, The Chargers Best Hide."

But the Broncos' coach also said, "It is a nice feeling to finally have the first winning season in the history of the franchise. It's good to be going into the 14th game of the year next weekend fighting for a division championship."

Reminded that the defeat handed the Chargers their worst season ever, Ralston replied, "Is that right? Well, you certainly have to give them credit. They didn't quit, they never gave up. Jerry LeVias had a fine day. Ron Smith was dangerous running back those kickoffs, and Gary Garrison is always tough."

Ralston admitted his team was a little tight in the early going because of the importance of the game. "We talked it over at halftime and decided just what we had to do to pull ourselves together."

Running back Floyd Little, whose name belies his many accomplishments, was feeling, "Super, that's all, just super," over finally being with a winner after several lean seasons.

Charger coach Ron Waller was bitter over the continuing mistakes which plague his club. "You can't have punts blocked, you can't fail to field punts and do a lot of other things like that," he argued. "We beat ourselves again."

Waller admitted he was second-guessing when the Chargers tried to run the ball off field goal formation from the Denver 13 on the last play of the first half. "I suppose since it didn't work I wouldn't do it again," he confessed, "but as it turned out, it really didn't make that much difference."

Even when the Chargers score, they or their fans seem to suffer. Celebrating a first-half San Diego touchdown, Bob Crull fired the Charger cannon and wound up in University Hospital with third degree burns on his hand and arm. He wasn't the only casualty. Charger fans have been doing a slow burn all season.

"We just got tired of losing this season," he explained. "We started all pulling together. I think that Monday night game, when we tied Oakland, was when we turned it around. But we should have won our division by now. We shouldn't have lost to the 49ers. We shouldn't have tied St. Louis. We have a great team this year," Little continued. "Charley Johnson is a super quarterback, real smart. And he can really read those zones. We have good players all the way down the line," he insisted and named a dozen or so in rapid succession.

Little also credits Ralston with bringing the team together. "He never says an unkind word. He never swears. Once in a while he gets mad and says 'Doggone It' or something like that. But when he really gets mad, his eyes get red, and then you better watch out."

RAIDERS SNIFFED RALSTON'S ROSE BOWL GADGET

by Bob Valli,
Oakland Tribune

John Ralston's fourth quarter blunder helped end for 1973 hi hopes of an "inevitable" Super Bowl for the Denver Broncos.

With Oakland leading 14-10, bu Denver's defense holding the Raiders without a second-half first down, the Broncos had a fourth-and-ten at their own 49.

By the book, it was time to punt Oakland into a hole and hold ground for solid field position on a return boot.

But Ralston went to his gimmick bag, not unexpectedly, and used a gadget play that worked for him at Stanford in the 1972 Rose Bowl against Michigan. He called a fake punt.

But this was the NFL with the AFC West championship on the line and the play backfired. Joe Dawkins, unlike Jackie Brown against the Wolverines at Pasadena, was buried under the Rose Coliseum turf by Joe Carroll and Monte Johnson for 7 yard loss.

Three plays later the Raiders scored and even a gift touchdown, handed them by Marv Hubbard's fumble at the Oakland 11, couldn't save the Broncos.

"There was a hole so big it scared you to death," said Ralston while wiping away the tears with a soaked handkerchief. "The fake punt started with an inside reverse and was a sweep right. It would have worked except we had a bad snap.

The play was designed for rookie Otis Armstrong to take a handoff from Dawkins and then to the outside. But Armstrong's appearance on the punting team for the first time was a giveaway.

"I yelled 'new guy, new guy, look for it outside' when I saw Armstrong go in there," explained Carroll. "Instead Dawkins just came at me."

John Madden had it figured too. "We keyed the run, not the punt in that situation," said the Oakland coach. "We had the lock on, keeping our players on the line instead of turning downfield. There was no element of surprise. Denver had tried it too often in the past. We stressed the fake punt all week in practice. It wouldn't have worked if the snap was good."

Armstrong disagreed. "It was a new wrinkle, something we hadn't tried all season but had worked on in practice every week," said the rookie from Purdue. "There was nobody out there where I was supposed to run, but the snap was low and when I saw Dawkins mishandle it, I new we'd blown it."

"It was the big surprise play but it turned the game around instead," he continued. "It was a do or die situation and we had to gamble."

Dawkins explained why it went awry. "I couldn't pull the ball up into my hands, it was stuck in

my stomach," he said. "Otis went by me before I could get a grip and hand off so I just went on a dive. The play was there and it would have been a great play."

It wasn't a day for gimmicks. Denver opened the second half with an onside kickoff and, although it caught the Raiders by surprise, the ball didn't travel the necessary 10 yards to the 50.

"We did it to gain momentum," said Ralston. "We were facing an uphill battle and we had to make things happen." Ralston also tried to work the clock to Denver's advantage in the final two minutes. It was unsuccessful too.

"There was 2:39 left and I designated Charlie Greer as our field captain to call time out," he said. "But the officials wouldn't recognize him. I guess I didn't make myself clear. Then they let it run to two minutes which was nine seconds over the alloted time between plays. I didn't understand it. That's why I rushed out onto the field."

"We could have saved a time out then but Oakland beat us and it's a team that will make a fine representative of our division in the playoffs. You have to respect the Raiders and we certainly wish them the best and hope they win the Super Bowl.

Ralston gave his Broncos an emotional post-game speech, apparently so high-pitched he cried. "I told 'em how proud I was of the tremendous effort they gave all season. Every guy gave 110 per cent of himself. We had no loafers. We'll be back again."

Soon Ralston will have the weapons to play it straight. Then he can forget about that strategic surprise that often boomerangs.

A few days before the 1975 NFL All-Star game in Miami, Riley Odoms was relaxing at AFC head-quarters, the Americana Hotel.

"There's lots of reasons," the best tight end in football said, discussing Denver's disappointing season. "We had a tough schedule, especially the first few games. We were inconsistent, very inconsistent. But the biggest single factor was not having Paul Smith. . .

"We're a different team without Paul. When the defense finally adjusted to not having him around, it was too late. His absence hurt the offense too. I believe we could have made the playoffs, maybe not the division title, but at least the wild card, with Paul healthy."

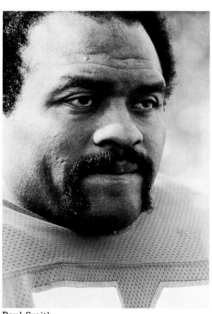

Paul Smith

Denver's offensive line held open house for Los Angeles' aggressors as Ram rushers ruined the Broncos' 1974 debut will a 17-10 opening day victory.

LA scored 10 points in the second quarter on Ray Guy's 19-yard field goal and John Hadl's 19-yard pass to Bob Klein. After Jim Turner's third-quarter three pointer, ex-CU star Cullen Bryant raced 84 yards to give the Rams a two-touchdown lead. Charley Johnson's 30-yard TD pass to Bill Van Heusen with less than three minutes left to play completed the scoring.

"It looked like a Super Bowl," local analysts commented about Denver's first-ever season debut against a NFL team. "Both teams were too cautious, afraid to make mistakes."

In 1973 the Rams led the NFC in scoring, posting a 12-2 record and Chuck Knox was Conference Coach of the Year. In 1974 LA won five of six exhibition games and was picked to win their division easily.

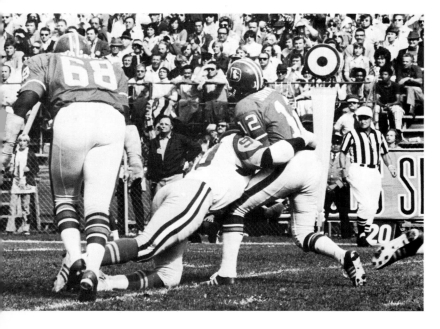

But the Rams carefully concealed their explosive offense. Hadl ignored free downs, choosing to run for short yardage rather than gamble on a long gain. In the second half LA's only offense was Bryant's kickoff return.

One-time Bronco boss Ray Malavasi used his multiple defensive systems against Denver. The Broncos gained only 52 yards rushing and 144 yards passing. Charley Johnson was sacked six times and the Ram defense stopped Denver cold on 13 third-down and two fourth-down situations.

The Broncos started 1974 with high hopes. In 1973 Denver led the AFC in scoring en route to their first winning season in history. John Ralston was also voted Conference Coach of the Year. Denver was 4-2 in pre-season and was expected to challenge Oakland's recent dominance over the AFC Western division.

Denver's scoring punch was even less impressive than Los Angeles'. The Broncos' 13 offensive series were uncomplicated, unimaginative and unproductive. Five plays and punt. Five plays and punt. Three plays and punt. Three plays and punt. Three plays and punt. Halftime. Three plays and punt. Four plays and punt. Six plays—field goal. Six plays and punt. Five plays—lose ball on downs. Three plays and punt. Four plays—touchdown. Five plays—lose ball on downs.

Denver's Paul Smith-less defense spent more than 40 minutes on the field. Ray May, Tom Jackson and John Grant combined for 23 tackles and four assists. Charles Greer made the game's lone interception.

"We were lethargic," said John Ralston. "I think we met a very good team today, but I'm disappointed in the way we started out."

The Pittsburgh Steelers, unable to beat Denver in three previous meetings, had to settle for a 35-35 tie in one of Mile High Stadium's longest and most exciting Sunday afternoons.

The Broncos led 21-7 after the 56-minute first quarter. "I looked up once thinking we were deep in the second quarter," Ken Criter told Dick Conner, "And there was still seven minutes left in the first."

Joe Gilliam led the Steelers to four second-half touchdowns. After Charley Johnson wrenched a shoulder, reliever Steve Ramsey threw touchdown passes three yards to Riley Odoms and 23 yards to Otis Armstrong to tie the score at 35.

With five seconds left in the game Bill Thompson raced around Pittsburgh's left side to deflect Ray Gerela's 25-yard field-goal attempt. The new NFL tie-breaker rule went into effect.

"Those of you smart enough to sneak away early," chided KOA announcer Bob Martin, "Can listen to the fifth quarter on your car radios."

Denver lost their third consecutive coin toss of 1974 and kicked to Pittsburgh. The Steelers used six minutes before John Rowser intercepted Gilliam's 50th pass and returned it to Denver's 42.

Ramsey and Otis Armstrong gobbled up time and yardage. After an aborted statue-of-liberty play the Broncos had fourth down at Pittsburgh's 24. Jim Turner, whose five extra points put him over the 1,000-point career mark, lined up from the 31 with 3:13 left in overtime. His kick floated wide.

Two physically and emotionally exhausted teams played out the final few minutes of NFL history's first regular-season overtime game.

Despite Floyd Little's promise that, "We will beat the Redskins," Washington embarrassed the Broncos 30-3 on ABC's Monday Night Circus.

Denver mistakes gave George Allen's ageless wonders a 13-0 halftime lead. Jim Turner's third-quarter field goal was Denver's only score. The Redskins added 17 points in the fourth quarter, including a last-second touchdown which Washington stopped the clock to score.

"I thought calling a timeout was a no-class act," fumed Charley Johnson. "I was embarrassed for the NFL as well as for us. I told Allen so on the field afterward."

Johnson and Denver's offense had a rough night against Washington's stingy defense. Charley completed 11 of 22 passes for 112 yards. The running game netted a mere 53 yards.

"I don't have any ready explanation," John Ralston said. "We'll just have to suck it up a little, admit we laid an egg in the big one, and then test ourselves to see what we're made of."

On the American Football League's 200th weekend Denver snapped a 14-year jinx and beat Kansas City for the first time ever on the road. John Ralston and relief quarterback Steve Ramsey credited the Bronco defense with the 17-14 victory.

Charley Johnson injured his thumb in pre-game warmups and was ineffective in the first half. Bobby Bell returned a Johnson interception 28 yards for a touchdown to give the Chiefs a 14-3 lead at intermission.

Ramsey replaced Johnson and directed Denver to two TDs. Jon Keyworth scored both on short plunges. Ramsey completed four of nine passes for 63 yards.

"I've never been associated with a more bitter loss," said Chief coach Hank Stram. "What happened to our offense in the second half was unbelievable."

What happened to their offense was Denver's defense. Tom Jackson made 14 tackles and two assists; Lyle Alzado had three tackles, three assists and two sacks; Calvin Jones stopped a Kansas City comeback attempt with a key interception.

Floyd Little, who picked up 81 yards rushing and receiving passes, agreed with Ralston and Ramsey's praise of the defense. "The defense changed the tempo of the game," said Little. "They took control of the game. I saw it when we walked on the field after the first series of the second half."

It was Denver's first win of 1974.

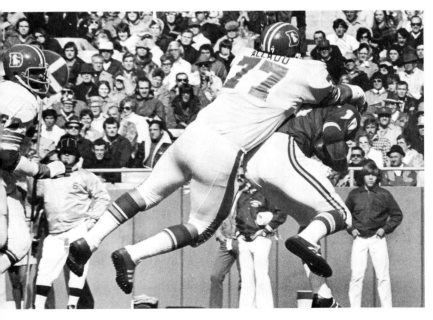

Steve Ramsey completed 17 of 27 passes for 295 yards and two touchdowns to beat New Orleans 33-17. The victory gave Denver second place in the AFC West with a 2-2-1 record. It was the Saints' 19th straight road loss.

The Broncos, betting favorites for the first time in 1974, rolled up almost 400 yards against New Orleans' unimpressive defense.

"Not much to say," Archie Manning told reporters. "We didn't do anything and I'm tired of trying to think up reasons why we're not winning. We were able to move the ball, then we had breakdowns on crucial plays. . . I'm tired of getting beat."

Manning's disappointment was understandable. The Saints' defense, with two interceptions, scored 14 points. The offense, on a 52-yard Bill McClard field goal, scored only three points.

After Denver's second straight victory John Ralston said, "It's nice to win . . . but it was awful ragged."

The Broncos made it three in a row with a 27-7 romp over San Diego.

"It was a day of comebacks," a sports columnist noted. "Although in neither case should it have been necessary for the veteran stars to feel they had to prove anything."

He was referring to Charley Johnson and Floyd Little. Charley hit nine of 12 passes for 146 yards and one touchdown. Floyd rushed and caught passes for 194 yards and another score.

After beating the Chargers, the Broncos anxiously awaited news of the Cincinnati-Oakland game.

The Bengals led 27-23 late in the fourth quarter. But Ken Stabler took the Raiders 52 yards to a game-winning touchdown with eight seconds left in the game.

Stabler's heroics kept Oakland 1½ games ahead of the surging Broncos.

The Broncos' three-game winning streak and the Browns' four-game losing streak ended simultaneously when Cleveland captured a thrilling, come-from-behind 23-21 victory.

"It reminded me of a one-sided fight," wrote Leonard Cahn. "One warrior has his opponent stretched out on the canvas in almost every round and is so far out in front as the final stanza starts he has a unanimous decision assured. But then the battered opponent, only intent on lasting the distance, suddenly winds up and connects with a one-punch haymaker for a knockout."

Charley Johnson completed 14 of 27 passes for 207 yards and two touchdowns. Otis Armstrong rushed 17 times for 142 yards—almost twice Cleveland's total rushing yardage. Denver's defense, despite Brown first downs at the Bronco 14, 20 and eight, allowed only nine points through the first three quarters.

The defense stifled Mike Phipps, forcing the Browns to bring in rookie quarterback Brian Sipe for the "final stanza." Sipe somehow scored two touchdowns while the Broncos twiddled their chinstraps on offense and defense.

"We were too conservative at spots," understated John Ralston. "I have no explanation for what happened today except to say it won't happen again. We will have to learn to score a knockout when we have a team in trouble."

When Jim Turner's desperate 51-yard field goal attempt fell far short, the game was over. So was the 1974 season.

"The Raiders have been the yardstick of excellence in our division the last few years," admitted John Ralston prior to a semi-showdown in Denver. "Obviously it will take a supreme effort on our part to win the game. Our battle plan has change since losing to Cleveland, but we always figured we were going to have to beat Oakland to have a shot at the title."

Ken Stabler's four TD passes upset Ralston's "battle plan" and gave Oakland a 28-17 victory. Charley Johnson statistically out-passed the classy southpaw, but the Broncos were unable to seriously threaten Oakland's inevitable trip to the playoffs.

Denver's defense did not play badly in the chilly confines of Mile High Stadium. Ray May and Lyle Alzado combined for 16 tackles and nine assists. But Marv Hubbard's 107 yards by land complimented Stabler's aerial act to keep the Raiders just out of reach.

Trailing 21-10 the Broncos battled back to a four-point deficit when Johnson and Bill Van Heusen connected for a 73-yard score. Minutes later Stabler hit Branch with a 61-yard TD bomb.

While John Madden and his troops celebrated their seventh straight win, Bronco fans filed out of their snow-covered seats in silence.

Denver visited Baltimore needing six straight victories to earn a shot at the wild card playoff spot. In a game neither team deserved to win, the Broncos beat the Colts 17-6.

Otis Armstrong gained 120 of Denver's 171 total yards. Wounded Colt quarterback Marty Domres led his team to 323 yards—doubling Denver's offensive output.

Bronco defenders, notably Barney Chavous, Lyle Alzado, Ray May, Randy Gradishar and Bill Thompson, were just tough enough. The Colts could only convert their impressive offensive statistics into two short field goals.

"It was a learning game," said John Ralston, "But lousy as Hell. We did get to see a lot more people, and saw some things that will require a lot of mulling over and some deep thought."

Given a choice between *Monday Night Football* and *The Godfather,* most of the nation's television viewers picked Marlon Brando. Only an estimated 10% of the entire television audience watched Denver and Kansas City pile up 896 yards and 76 points in an offensive thriller. The Broncos won the battle for yardage but lost the game 42-34.

Charley Johnson completed 28 of 42 passes for 445 yards and two touchdowns. Len Dawson hit 19 of 30 passes for 188 yards and two TDs.

Bronco rookie runner Jon Keyworth scored three touchdowns. Rookie Woody Green gained 114 yards rushing and scored once for the Chiefs.

Riley Odoms rambled 125 yards with seven Johnson passes. Haven Moses and Otis Armstrong made another half-dozen receptions each.

The Broncos set five team offensive records with 532 total yards, 34 first downs, 459 yards passing, 25 first downs passing, and 58 first downs by both teams.

"It reminded me of the old American Football League," said Dawson, "Except the Broncos weren't wearing striped socks."

It was Kansas City's 26th victory in 30 games against Denver. Some Bronco fans wished they had watched *The Godfather*.

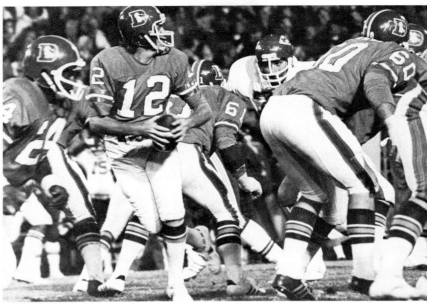

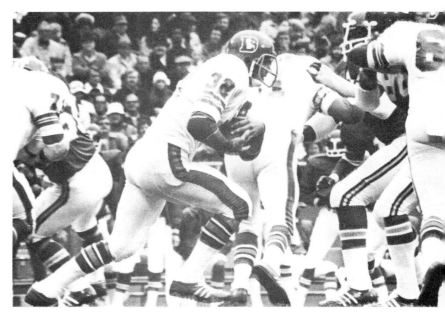

The Broncos stopped Oakland's nine-game winning streak 20-17. Jon Keyworth, Otis Armstrong and Denver's offensive line combined for a team rushing record 292 yards. It was suggested the Raiders were looking ahead to the playoffs.

"We recognize they may have been a little flat," commented coach Ralston. "I'm looking forward to the day they are at full strength and we are at full strength, and we're playing for the whole deal. It's not far off."

Ralston may be right. The young Broncos looked good against Oakland. Armstrong and Keyworth, along with Riley Odoms, Claudie Minor, Randy Gradishar, Jim O'Malley, Tom Jackson, and others enjoyed a fine day against the Raiders. They should all still be around when Ralston's prophecy comes true.

The Broncos celebrated Thanksgiving by beating Detroit 31-27. It was Denver's third game in 11 days and the third national television appearance of 1974 for Big Orange.

Otis Armstrong raced 144 yards, making him the season's first 1,000-yarder. Jon Keyworth added 61 yards and scored twice. It was the second straight 200-yard rushing day for Denver's dynamic backfield duo.

"Me and him are always together," Armstrong said about Keyworth. "He seems to like me."

Charley Johnson, who threw his first pro TD in Tiger Stadium, connected on 12 of 20 passes for 130 yards and one touchdown.

Trailing 17-10, Denver started the second half with a successful onside kick. "We watched it all week on films," said special-team coach Myrel Moore. "We knew it was open."

Six plays later Keyworth scored the first of Denver's three third-quarter touchdowns.

The loss knocked Detroit out of the playoff picture. The Broncos flew home to enjoy ten days of rest before completing the season against Houston and San Diego.

tis Armstrong gained 183 yards,
Bronco record, and scored three
ouchdowns as Denver defeated
Houston 37-14.

I wish we were at the other end,"
enter Bobby Maples commented,
With one game gone and 13
till to play."

Denver's offense was awesome
gain. The Broncos amassed
most 1,500 yards in successive
ames against Kansas City, Oak-
and, Detroit and Houston. In
hose games Armstrong rushed for
30 yards, bringing his season
otal to 1,265 (also a Bronco
ecord) and virtually assuring
urdue's powerhouse the NFL
ushing championship.

he victory gave Denver its second
traight winning season. John
Ralston was happy with the win
s he looked ahead to San Diego.

We want to finish with four in a
ow and with eight wins for the
irst time in Bronco history," the
oach told Bob Collins. "That will
ive us the momentum going into
ext year when, hopefully, we
von't let some early lapses keep
s out of the playoffs."

"I just flat did a lousy job of
preparing them," mumbled John
Ralston. He has made that
statement before. This time it
followed a humiliating 17-0 loss
to San Diego.

The lackluster Broncos were
unable to score on the AFC's
worst defensive team. Charger
scores resulted directly from
Denver mistakes. So much
for momentum.

Only Otis Armstrong's 142 yards
and NFL rushing crown glowed
on an otherwise dark afternoon
for Bronco fans. It was a
frustrating end to a frustrating
season, but John Ralston and
Denver will be back.
You can bet on it.

THE POINT AFTER

Some say statistics
are for losers.
This is no longer
true for the
Denver Broncos...

1960

1960 DENVER BRONCOS

Front row (left to right) — Lionel Taylor, Jim Greer, Henry Bell, John Brodnax, Bob Stransky, David Rolle, Bob McNamara, Skip Doyle, Buddy Alliston. Second row — Assistant Coach Jim Cason, Al Carmichael, Albert Day, Pete Mangum, John Pyeatt, Frank Tripucka, George Herring, Gordie Holz, Assistant Coach Dale Dodrill. Third row — Head Coach Frank Filchock, Frank Kuchta, Gene Mingo, Willie Smith, Ken Adamson, Mike Nichols, Goose Gonsoulin, Bud McFadin. Fourth row — Trainer and Equipment Manager Fred Posey, Eldon Danenhauer, Don King, Carl Larpenter, John Hatley, Charles Gavin, Ed Work, Dave Strickland, Joseph Young. Fifth row — General Manager Dean Griffing, Bill Danenhauer, Jim O'Donnell, Bill Jessup, Hardy Brown, Tom McMahon, Don Allen, Albert Romine. Top row — Bill Rogers, Harold Smith, Bill Yelverton, Bob Crabtree, Frank Bernardi.

PRE-SEASON (0-5-0)

6 Boston 43 (Providence, R.I.)
14 Buffalo 31 (Rochester)
3 at Houston 42
0 Dallas 48 (Little Rock)
30 at Los Angeles 36

REGULAR SEASON (4-9-1)

13 at Boston 10
27 at Buffalo 21
24 at New York 28
31 Oakland 14
19 Los Angeles 23
31 Boston 24
14 Dallas 17
25 Houston 45
7 at Dallas 34
10 at Houston 20
38 Buffalo 38
27 New York 30
33 at Los Angeles 41
10 at Oakland 48

BRONCO ALL-TIME TEAM RECORDS

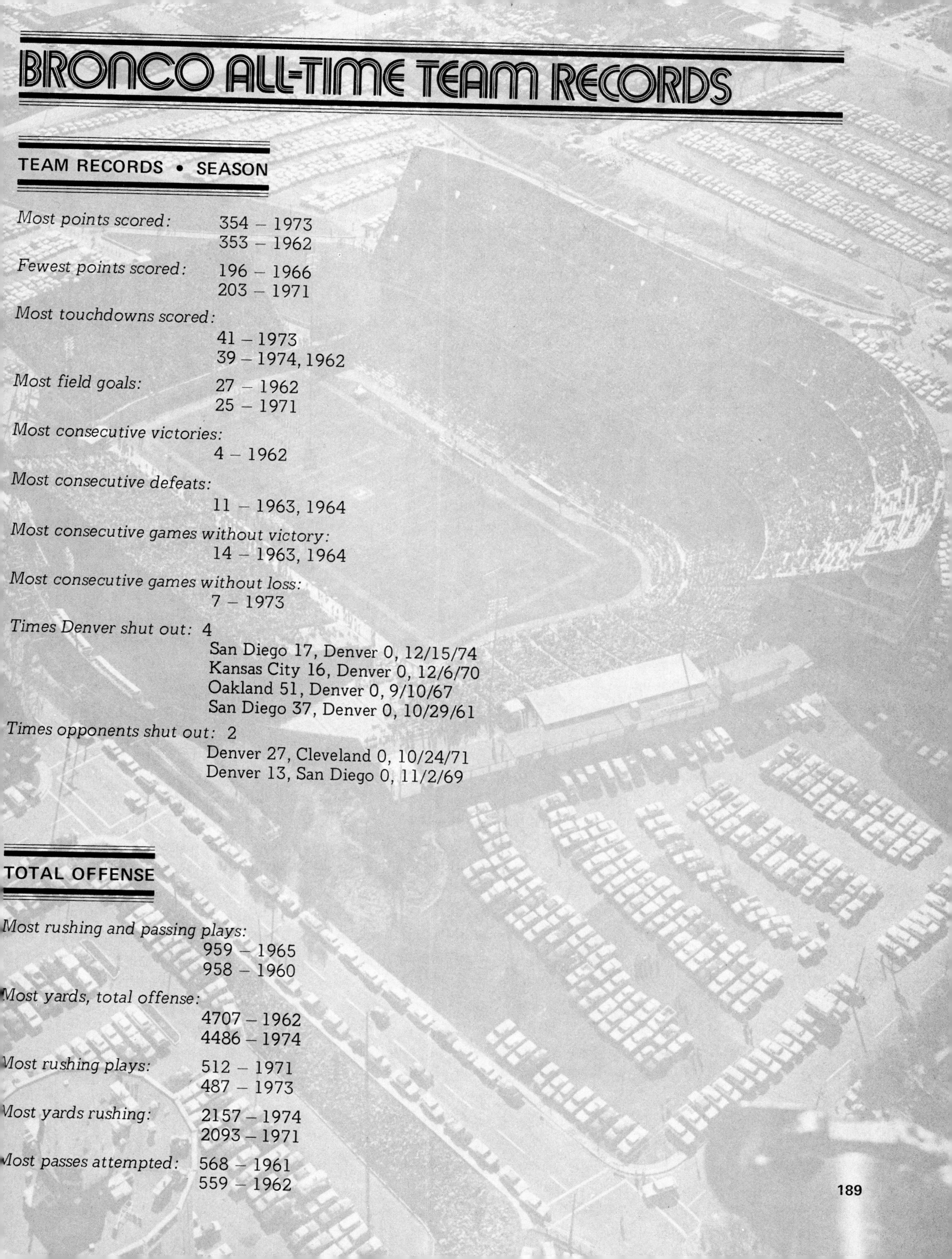

TEAM RECORDS • SEASON

Most points scored: 354 — 1973
353 — 1962

Fewest points scored: 196 — 1966
203 — 1971

Most touchdowns scored:
41 — 1973
39 — 1974, 1962

Most field goals: 27 — 1962
25 — 1971

Most consecutive victories:
4 — 1962

Most consecutive defeats:
11 — 1963, 1964

Most consecutive games without victory:
14 — 1963, 1964

Most consecutive games without loss:
7 — 1973

Times Denver shut out: 4
San Diego 17, Denver 0, 12/15/74
Kansas City 16, Denver 0, 12/6/70
Oakland 51, Denver 0, 9/10/67
San Diego 37, Denver 0, 10/29/61

Times opponents shut out: 2
Denver 27, Cleveland 0, 10/24/71
Denver 13, San Diego 0, 11/2/69

TOTAL OFFENSE

Most rushing and passing plays:
959 — 1965
958 — 1960

Most yards, total offense:
4707 — 1962
4486 — 1974

Most rushing plays: 512 — 1971
487 — 1973

Most yards rushing: 2157 — 1974
2093 — 1971

Most passes attempted: 568 — 1961
559 — 1962

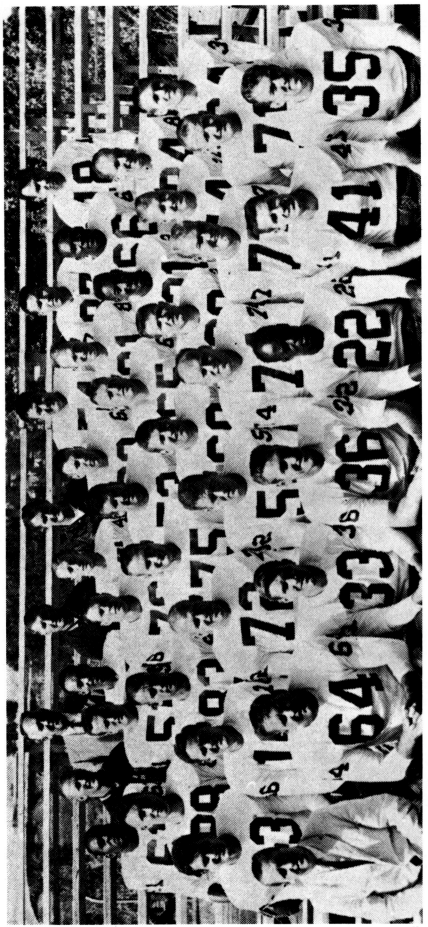

1961 DENVER BRONCOS

Front row (left to right) — President Calvin Kunz, Jr., Bud McFadin, Fred Bukaty, Jim Stinnette, Buddy Allen, Bob McNamera, Jim Sears. Second row — Goose Gonsoulin, George Herring, Jerry Sturm, Jim Barton, Gordy Holz, Carl Larpenter, Art Hauser. Third row — Gene Prebola, Johnny Pyeatt, Eldon Danenhauer, Ken Adamson, Jerry Traynham, Dan Smith, Don Stone. Fourth row — Chuck Gavin, Mike Nichols, Jack Mattox, Bob Hudson, Joe Young, Gene Mingo, Jack Hill. Fifth row — Assistant Coach Ken Carpenter, Al Frazier, Jim McMillin, Jim Elfrid, Laneair Roberts, John Cash. Sixth row — General Manager Dean Griffing, Head Coach Frank Filchock, Assistant Coach Dale Dodrill, Wahoo McDaniel, Lionel Taylor, Frank Tripucka.

PRE-SEASON (1-4-0)

13 at Dallas 31 (Midland, Tex.)
48 Oakland 21   (Spokane)
27 at Dallas 29 (Ft. Worth)
10 Houston 42   (Mobile)
12 at Oakland 49

REGULAR SEASON (3-11-0)

22 at Buffalo 10
17 at Boston 45
28 at New York 35
19 at Oakland 33
12 Dallas 19
27 Oakland 24
27 New York 10
0 at San Diego 37
14 Houston 55
16 San Diego 19
10 Buffalo 23
14 at Houston 45
24 Boston 28
21 at Dallas 49

Most passes completed:
292 – 1962
265 – 1961

Most passes intercepted:
45 – 1961
40 – 1962

Most touchdown passes:
24 – 1960
23 – 1969, 1963

Most yards passing:
3404 – 1962
3247 – 1960

Fewest yards passing:
1682 – 1967
1995 – 1966

Fewest times Denver QB sacked:
22 – 1971 (178 yds)
24 – 1965 (208 yds)

Most times Denver QB sacked:
63 – 1963 (590 yds)
58 – 1967 (508 yds)

Most first downs:
270 – 1962
258 – 1974

Most first downs rushing:
120 – 1974
111 – 1973, 1965

Most first downs passing:
177 – 1962
141 – 1960

Most first downs by penalties:
27 – 1965
26 – 1969

Most punts:
105 – 1967
96 – 1968

Fewest punts:
59 – 1962
60 – 1972

Best punting average:
45.2 – 1966
45.1 – 1973

Poorest punting average:
37.3 – 1960
39.3 – 1961

Most punt returns:
63 – 1970
43 – 1974

Most yards, punt returns:
556 – 1970
474 – 1974

Best average, punt returns:
13.5 – 1967
12.2 – 1969

Most kickoff returns:
78 – 1963
75 – 1964

1962 DENVER BRONCOS

Front row (left to right) — Bo Dickinson, Don Stone, Goose Gonsoulin, Bob Zeman, Jim Stinnette, Jim McMillin, Al Frazier. Second row — Tom Minter, Charles Marshall, John McGeever, Jerry Sturm, Bob Scarpitto, Justin Rowland, Carl Larpenter. Third row — George Shaw, Jerry Tarr, Jim Fraser, Jerry Stalcup, Bill Roehnelt, Don Joyce, Gene Mingo, Gordy Holz. Fourth row — Frank Tripucka, John Denvir, Gene Prebola, Lionel Taylor, John Cash, Wahoo McDaniel, Bud McFadin, Chuck Gavin. Fifth row — Ike Lassiter, Larry Jordan, Jim Barton, Eldon Danenhauer, Ken Adamson, Jim Perkins, Bob McCullough, Hunter Enis. Sixth row — Assistant Coach Mac Speedie, Assistant Coach Gary Glick, General Manager and Head Coach Jack Faulkner, Assistant Coach Jim Martin, Assistant Coach Dale Dodrill, Trainer Fred Posie.

PRE-SEASON (2-2-0)

17 Houston 33 (Atlanta)
24 at San Diego 31
27 at Dallas 24
41 at Oakland 12 (Stockton)

REGULAR SEASON (7-7-0)

30 San Diego 21
23 at Buffalo 20
16 at Boston 41
32 at New York 10
44 Oakland 7
23 at Oakland 6
20 Houston 10
38 Buffalo 45
23 at San Diego 20
29 Boston 33
3 Dallas 24
45 New York 46
17 at Houston 34
10 at Dallas 17

Most yards, kickoff returns:
                1801 — 1963
                1758 — 1964

Best average, kickoff returns:
                26.8 — 1966
                25.3 — 1967

Most fumbles: 40 — 1961
                36 — 1966

Most fumbles lost: 23 — 1961
                17 — 1966, 1960

Fewest fumbles: 15 — 1969
                20 — 1974

Fewest fumbles lost: 8 — 1969, 1964
                9 — 1973

Most penalties: 94 — 1970
                89 — 1972

Most yards penalized: 887 — 1970
                827 — 1972

Fewest penalties: 48 — 1967
                54 — 1960

Fewest yards penalized:
                501 — 1960
                512 — 1967

TOTAL DEFENSE

Fewest rushes allowed: 384 — 1965
                409 — 1970

Fewest yards allowed: 1337 — 1965
                1351 — 1970

Fewest passing attempts allowed:
                379 — 1970
                386 — 1960

Fewest completions allowed:
                150 — 1971
                188 — 1960

Fewest net yards allowed:
                1986 — 1971
                2192 — 1972

Fewest TD passes allowed:
                14 — 1974
                16 — 1973

Most interceptions: 32 — 1964
                28 — 1967

Most yards, interceptions returned:
                483 — 1962
                465 — 1965

1963 DENVER BRONCOS

Front row (left to right) — Head Coach Jack Faulkner, Tom Rychlec, Gene Mingo, Charles Gavin, Eldon Danenhauer, Bud McFadin, Wahoo McDaniel, Gordie Holz, Assistant Coach Mac Speedie. Second row — Assistant Coach Red Miller, Ray Jacobs, Anton Peters, Willie Brown, Ike Lassiter, John Nocera, Bob McCullough, Billy Joe, Trainer Allen Hurst. Third row — Assistant Coach Ed Hughes, Jim Perkins, Bill Groman, Bob Zeman, Jim Fraser, Tom Erlandson, Gene Prebola, Goose Gonsoulin, Ernie Barnes. Fourth row — Player Personnel Director Ray Malavasi, Charlie Mitchell, John McGeever, Don Coffey, Tom Janik, Mickey Slaughter, Tom Nomina, John McCormick, Jerry Hopkins. Fifth row — Assistant Trainer Max Morton, Don Breaux, Don Stone, Bob Scarpitto, Lionel Taylor, Jerry Sturm, Hewritt Dixon, Harold Olson, Assistant Coach Dale Dodrill.

PRE-SEASON (2-3-0)

27 Houston 10
19 at Oakland 35
31 San Diego 25
16 at Kansas City 30
14 Buffalo 21 (Winston-Salem)

REGULAR SEASON (2-11-1)

7 Kansas City 59
14 at Houston 20
14 Boston 10
50 San Diego 34
24 Houston 33
21 at Boston 40
35 at New York 35
28 Buffalo 30
17 at Buffalo 27
9 New York 14
10 Oakland 26
21 at Kansas City 52
31 at Oakland 35
20 at San Diego 58

Most times opponents' QB sacked:
                    50 — 1970
                    45 — 1969
Most yardage opponents' QB thrown for losses:
                    456 — 1970
                    447 — 1964
Most opponents' fumbles recovered:
                    21 — 1964
                    20 — 1971, 1963
Fewest opponents' fumbles recovered:
                    11 — 1974
                    12 — 1972, 1968

Fewest opponents' first downs:
                    199 — 1970
                    206 — 1971
Fewest opponents' first downs rushing:
                    67 — 1970
                    83 — 1971
Fewest opponents' first downs passing:
                    91 — 1971
                    118 — 1970
Fewest opponents' first downs on penalties:
                    12 — 1968
                    14 — 1970
Most opponents' penalties:
                    98 — 1961
                    86 — 1965
Most yards opponents penalized:
                    901 — 1969
                    837 — 1973
Fewest points allowed: 264 — 1970
                    275 — 1971
Fewest touchdowns allowed:
                    28 — 1970
                    31 — 1973
Fewest field goals allowed:
                    13 — 1961
                    14 — 1965

TEAM RECORDS • SINGLE GAME

Most points scored: 50 — vs. San Diego, 10/6/63
                    48 — vs. Houston, 10/14/73
Largest margin of victory:
                    37 — vs. Oakland, 10/5/62 (44-7)
Most points, one half: 33 — vs. San Diego, 10/6/63
Most points, one quarter:
                    26 — vs. New York, 12/3/67

1964 DENVER BRONCOS

Front row (left to right) — Head Coach Mac Speedie, Willie Brown, John McGeever, Billy Joe, Jim McMillin, Goose Gonsoulin, Jerry Hopkins, Jim Fraser, Odell Barry, Defensive Line Coach Ray Malavasi. Second row — Offensive Coach Red Miller, Jacky Lee, Charlie Mitchell, Billy Atkins, Tom Janik, Harold Olson, Stan Fanning, Al Denson, Equipment Manager Chuck Ziober. Third row — Defensive Backfield Coach George Dickson, Wendell Hayes, Matt Snorton, Leroy Moore, Larry Jordan, Jim Price, Gary Henson, John Griffin, Ernie Barnes, Trainer Allen Hurst. Fourth row — Don Shackleford, Hewritt Dixon, Dick Guesman, Charlie Janerette, Ray Jacobs, Ed Cooke, Bob Scarpitto, Lionel Taylor. Fifth row — Marv Matuszak, Mickey Slaughter, Ray Kubala, Eldon Danenhauer, Jerry Sturm, Jim Perkins, Bob McCullough, Don Stone.

PRE-SEASON (2-3-0)

20 at San Diego 34
7 Oakland 20
32 at Houston 20
10 Kansas City 14 (Ft. Worth)
28 Boston 17

REGULAR SEASON (2-11-1)

6 at New York 30
13 at Buffalo 30
17 Houston 38
10 Boston 39
33 Kansas City 27
14 at San Diego 42
7 at Oakland 40
39 at Kansas City 49
20 San Diego 31
20 New York 16
7 at Boston 12
20 Oakland 20
19 Buffalo 30
15 at Houston 34

TOTAL OFFENSE

Most rushing and passing plays:

     84 — vs. Boston, 12/3/61

Most yards, total offense:

     532 — vs. Kansas City, 11/18/74

Most rushing plays: 57 — vs. Cleveland, 10/24/71

Most yards rushing: 292 — vs. Oakland, 11/24/74

Most passes attempted: 56 — vs. Boston, 9/21/62
     56 — vs. Buffalo, 9/15/62

Most passes completed: 35 — vs. Houston, 12/20/64

Most passes intercepted: 8 — vs. Houston, 12/2/62

Most yards passing: 459 — vs. Kansas City, 11/18/74

Most touchdown passes: 5 — vs. Buffalo, 10/28/62

Most times Denver QB sacked:

     11 — vs. Oakland, 11/5/67
     11 — vs. Buffalo, 12/13/64

Most first downs: 34 — vs. Kansas City, 11/18/74

Most first downs rushing:

     16 — vs. Boston, 9/24/65

Most first downs passing:

     25 — vs. Kansas City, 11/18/74

Most first downs penalties:

     6 — vs. Houston, 9/27/64

Most punts: 12 — vs. Cincinnati, 10/6/68
     12 — vs. Oakland, 9/10/67

Most punt returns: 8 — vs. Kansas City, 10/6/74
     8 — vs. Buffalo, 9/20/70

Most yards on punt returns:

     126 — vs. New York, 12/3/67

Most kickoff returns: 10 — vs. Boston, 10/4/64
     10 — vs. San Diego, 12/22/63

Most yards on kickoff returns:

     295 — vs. Boston, 10/4/64

Most fumbles: 6 — vs. Boston, 11/6/66
     6 — vs. Kansas City, 10/10/65
     6 — vs. Boston, 9/21/62
     6 — vs. Los Angeles, 10/16/60

Most fumbles lost: 5 — vs. Chicago, 9/30/73

Most penalties: 14 — vs. New York Jets, 10/28/73

Most yards penalized: 130 — vs. New York Titans, 11/22/62

Fewest penalties: 0 — vs. Kansas City, 12/17/67

Most field goals: 5 — vs. San Diego, 10/6/63

Fewest yards, total offense:

     5 — vs. Oakland, 9/10/67

1965

1965 DENVER BRONCOS

Front row (left to right) — Trainer Allen Hurst, Al Denson, Gary Kroner, Jim Thibert, Paul Carmichael, Odell Barry, John Bramlett, Willie Brown, Mickey Slaughter, Miller Farr, Ray Jacobs, Wendell Hayes, Offensive Backfield Coach Bus Mertes. Second row — Head Coach Mac Speedie, Offensive Coach Red Miller, Don Shackleford, Gerry Bussell, John McGeever, Nemiah Wilson, Charlie Parker, Tom Erlandson, Tom Nomina, Goose Gonsoulin, Hewritt Dixon, Jerry Hopkins, Cookie Gilchrist, Defensive Backfield Coach George Dixon, Charlie Mitchell. Third row — Equipment Manager Chuck Ziober, Jim Thompson, Ed Cooke, Max Leetzow, Jon Hohman, Bob Breitenstein, Bob McCullough, Eldon Danenhauer, Jerry Sturm, Ray Kubala, Jim McMillin, John McCormick, Darrell Lester, Linebacker Coach Marv Matuszak. Fourth row — Personnel Director Fred Gehrke, John Griffin, Alan Medley, Ed Cummings, Charlie Janerette, Lee Bernet, Jacky Lee, Leroy Moore, Gene Jeter, Lionel Taylor, Bob Scarpitto, Abner Haynes, Defensive Line Coach Ray Malavasi.

REGULAR SEASON (4-10-0)

31 at San Diego 34
15 Buffalo 30
27 at Boston 10
16 New York 13
23 Kansas City 31
28 Houston 17
13 at Buffalo 31
10 at New York 45
21 San Diego 35
31 at Houston 21
20 Oakland 28
13 at Oakland 24
20 Boston 28
35 at Kansas City 45

PRE-SEASON (1-4-0)

24 Kansas City 30
27 Oakland 17 (Salt Lake City)
6 San Diego 21
3 Houston 25 (San Antonio)
20 Oakland 30 (Sacramento)

Fewest yards rushing: 13 — vs. Cleveland, 10/22/72
Fewest yards passing: 6 — vs. New York, 11/15/64
Fewest first downs: 0 — vs. Houston, 9/3/66

TOTAL DEFENSE

Fewest total plays allowed:
                          40 — vs. San Diego, 10/6/63
Fewest yards allowed: 60 — vs. Cleveland, 10/24/71
Fewest rushing plays allowed:
                          11 — vs. New York Jets, 12/3/67
Fewest rushing yards allowed:
                          0 — vs. Kansas City, 12/19/65
Fewest passes allowed: 14 — vs. Kansas City, 11/27/69
                          14 — vs. Houston, 11/20/60
Fewest completions allowed:
                          5 — vs. Green Bay, 9/26/71
                          5 — vs. Dallas, 10/8/61
Fewest yards passing allowed:
                          7 — vs. Chicago, 12/5/71
Most interceptions: 6 — vs. Boston, 9/3/67
                          6 — vs. Houston, 11/14/65
                          6 — vs. New York, 11/15/64
                          6 — vs. Buffalo, 9/18/60
Most yards interceptions returned:
                          133 — at Buffalo, 9/18/60
Most times sacking opposing QB:
                          10 — vs. Cincinnati, 10/19/69
Fewest first downs allowed:
                          6 — vs. Cleveland, 10/24/71
                          6 — vs. Oakland, 11/20/66
Most fumbles caused: 7 — vs. Buffalo, 12/13/64
Most fumbles recovered:
                          5 — vs. Boston, 11/6/66
                          5 — vs. Buffalo, 12/13/64
                          5 — vs. Oakland, 10/14/62
Most yards opponent penalized:
                          140 — vs. Houston, 10/26/69
Fewest points scored by opponent:
                          0 — vs. Cleveland, 10/24/71
                          0 — vs. San Diego, 11/2/69

1966 DENVER BRONCOS

Front row (left to right) — Al Denson, Billy Ray Fletcher, Arch Matsos, Mickey Slaughter, Charlie Mitchell, Mike Kellogg, Bob Richardson, Abner Haynes, Pat Matson, Equipment Manager Larry Elliott. Second row — Assistant Coach Fred Gehrke, Eric Crabtree, Jerry Hopkins, Lewis Scott, Jon Hohman, Ron Sbranti, John Bramlett, Jerry Inman, Sam Brunelli, Jason Franci, Frank Rogers. Third row — Head Coach Ray Malavasi, Assistant Coach Marv Matuszak, Trainer Allen Hurst, Lonnie Wright, George Tarasovic, Max Leetzow, Lee Bernet, John Griffin, Darrell Lester, Bill Keating, Gary Kroner, Eugene Jeter, Assistant Coach Dale Dodrill, Assistant Coach Bus Mertes. Fourth row — Ray Jacobs, John Gonzaga, Dan LaRose, Max Choboian, Goose Gonsoulin, Jerry Sturm, Ray Kubala, Willie Brown, Larry Cox, Scotty Glacken, Goldie Sellers. Fifth row — Wendell Hayes, Larry Kaminski, John McCormick, Nemiah Wilson, Max Wettstein, Bob Young, Butch Davis.

PRE-SEASON (1-3-0)

30 Kansas City 32
3 at Buffalo 25
28 Miami 16 (Memphis)
21 Oakland 52

REGULAR SEASON (4-10-0)

7 at Houston 45
10 Boston 24
7 New York 16
40 Houston 38
10 at Kansas City 37
7 at Miami 24
10 Kansas City 56
17 at San Diego 24
17 at Boston 10
3 Oakland 17
20 San Diego 17
17 Miami 7
10 at Oakland 28
21 at Buffalo 38

Most rushing and passing plays:

- 1525 — Floyd Little
- 1283 — Frank Tripucka

Most yards gained:

- 7651 — Frank Tripucka
- 6212 — Charley Johnson

Most rushing plays:

- 1516 — Floyd Little
- 349 — Charlie Mitchell

Most yards gained rushing:

- 5878 — Floyd Little
- 1497 — Otis Armstrong

Most passes attempted:

- 1277 — Frank Tripucka
- 828 — Charley Johnson

Most passes completed:

- 662 — Frank Tripucka
- 452 — Charley Johnson

Most passes intercepted:

- 85 — Frank Tripucka
- 45 — Steve Tensi

Most touchdown passes:

- 51 — Frank Tripucka
- 47 — Charley Johnson

Most passes caught:

- 543 — Lionel Taylor
- 250 — Al Denson

Most yards gained on receptions:

- 6976 — Lionel Taylor
- 4132 — Al Denson

Most touchdown receptions:

- 44 — Lionel Taylor
- 33 — Al Denson

Most punts: 480 — Bill Van Heusen

Best average per punt:

- 45.2 — Jim Fraser
- 44.4 — Bob Scarpitto

Most passes intercepted:

- 43 — Goose Gonsoulin
- 19 — Bill Thompson

Most yards, interception returns:

- 542 — Goose Gonsoulin
- 445 — Bill Thompson

Most punt returns:

- 136 — Bill Thompson
- 81 — Floyd Little

Most yards, punt returns:

- 1591 — Bill Thompson
- 893 — Floyd Little

Most kickoff returns:

- 88 — Floyd Little
- 74 — Odell Barry

Most yards, kickoff returns:

- 2216 — Floyd Little
- 1856 — Odell Barry

Most touchdowns scored:

- 50 — Floyd Little
- 50 — Lionel Taylor

1967 DENVER BRONCOS

Front row (left to right) – Trainer Allen Hurst, Jerry Inman, Al Denson, Gene Sykes, Dave Costa, Pat Matson, Charlie Mitchell, John Huard, Equipment Manager Larry Elliott. Second row – Bob Scarpitto, Lonnie Wright, Jim Summers, Chip Myrtle, Goldie Sellers, Neal Sweeney, Rick Duncan, Jack Lentz, Floyd Little, Dave Behrman. Third row – Assistant Coach Stan Jones, Ron Sbranti, Ray Kubala, Larry Cox, Bill Keating, Frank Richter, Rex Mirich, Mike Current, Fran Lynch, Carl Cunningham, Henry Sorrell, Assistant Coach Whitey Dovell, Assistant Coach Dick MacPherson. Fourth row – Assistant Coach Sam Rutigliano, Rich Jackson, Bob Young, Sam Brunelli, Wendell Hayes, Jim Leclair, Tom Cichowski, Nemiah Wilson, Bo Hickey, Mike Kellogg, Pete Duranko, Dick Tyson, General Manager and Head Coach Lou Saban. Fifth row – Assistant Coach Hunter Enis, Lou Andrus, George Goeddeke, Andre White, Errol Prisby, Larry Kaminski, Steve Tensi, Tom Beer, Tom Cassese, Ernie Park, Max Choboian, Eric Crabtree.

PRE-SEASON (3-1-0)

2 Miami 19 (Akron)
13 Detroit 7
14 Minnesota 9
21 Oakland 17 (North Platte)

REGULAR SEASON (3-11-0)

26 Boston 21
0 at Oakland 51
21 at Miami 35
24 New York 38
6 at Houston 10
16 Buffalo 17
21 San Diego 33
9 at Kansas City 52
17 Oakland 21
18 Houston 20
21 at Buffalo 20
20 at San Diego 24
33 at New York 24
24 Kansas City 38

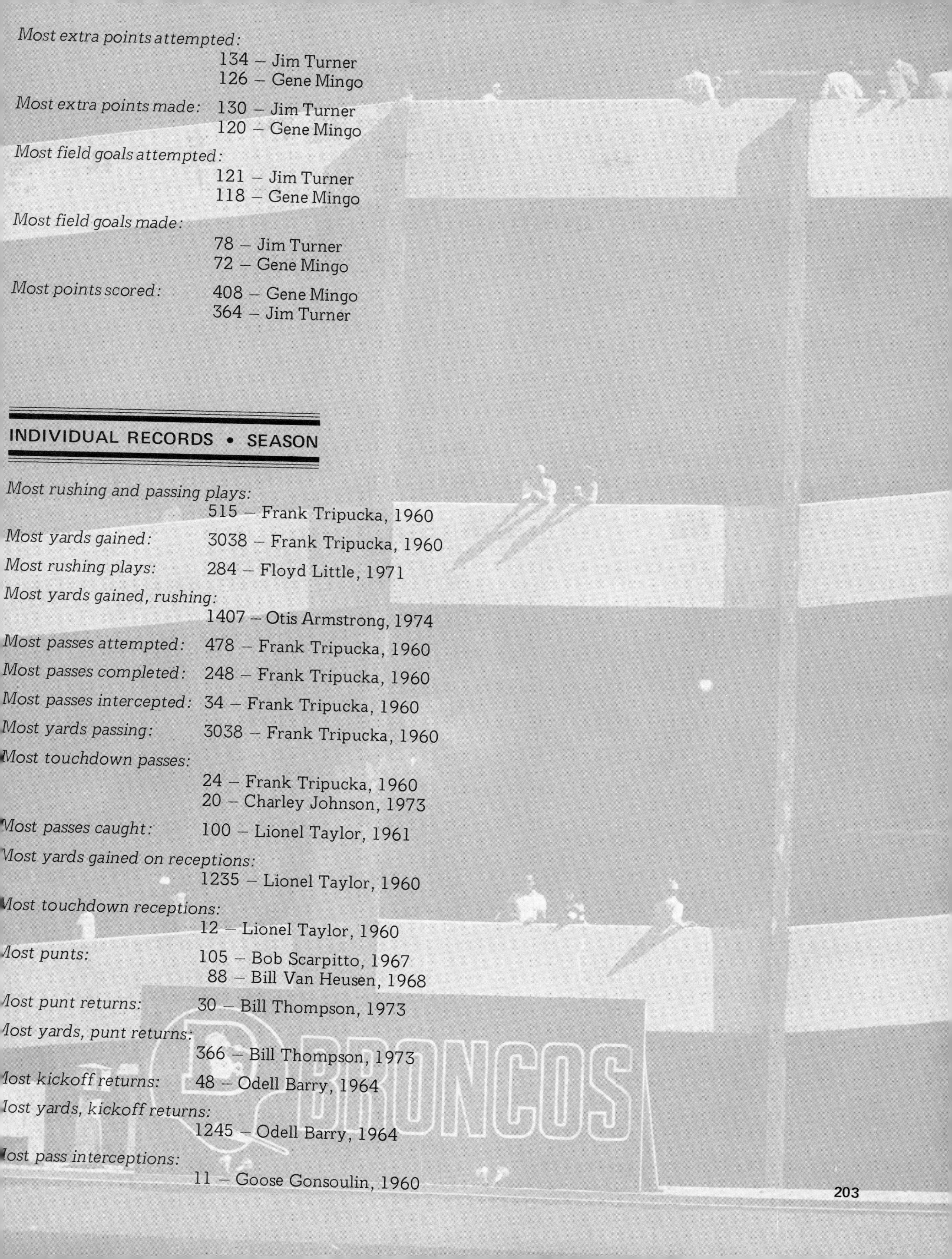

Most extra points attempted:
        134 — Jim Turner
        126 — Gene Mingo

Most extra points made: 130 — Jim Turner
        120 — Gene Mingo

Most field goals attempted:
        121 — Jim Turner
        118 — Gene Mingo

Most field goals made:
        78 — Jim Turner
        72 — Gene Mingo

Most points scored: 408 — Gene Mingo
        364 — Jim Turner

INDIVIDUAL RECORDS • SEASON

Most rushing and passing plays:
        515 — Frank Tripucka, 1960

Most yards gained: 3038 — Frank Tripucka, 1960

Most rushing plays: 284 — Floyd Little, 1971

Most yards gained, rushing:
        1407 — Otis Armstrong, 1974

Most passes attempted: 478 — Frank Tripucka, 1960

Most passes completed: 248 — Frank Tripucka, 1960

Most passes intercepted: 34 — Frank Tripucka, 1960

Most yards passing: 3038 — Frank Tripucka, 1960

Most touchdown passes:
        24 — Frank Tripucka, 1960
        20 — Charley Johnson, 1973

Most passes caught: 100 — Lionel Taylor, 1961

Most yards gained on receptions:
        1235 — Lionel Taylor, 1960

Most touchdown receptions:
        12 — Lionel Taylor, 1960

Most punts: 105 — Bob Scarpitto, 1967
        88 — Bill Van Heusen, 1968

Most punt returns: 30 — Bill Thompson, 1973

Most yards, punt returns:
        366 — Bill Thompson, 1973

Most kickoff returns: 48 — Odell Barry, 1964

Most yards, kickoff returns:
        1245 — Odell Barry, 1964

Most pass interceptions:
        11 — Goose Gonsoulin, 1960

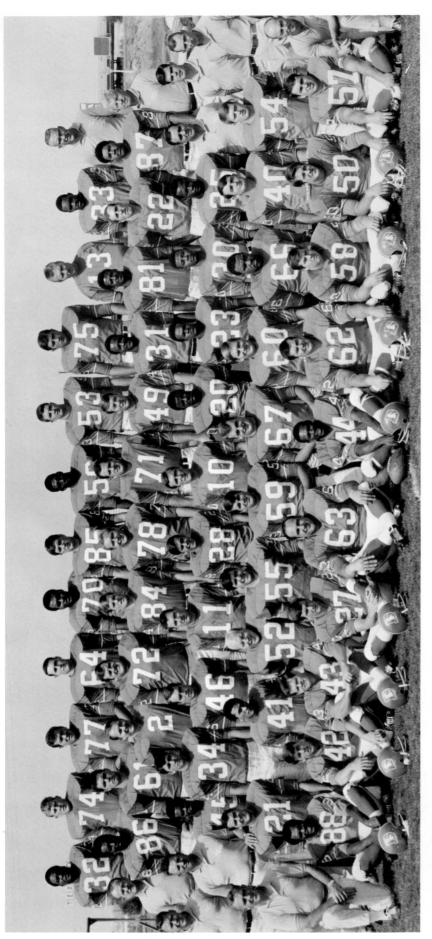

1968 DENVER BRONCOS

Front row (left to right) — Assistant Coach Dick MacPherson, Al Denson, Bill Van Heusen, Pete Jaquess, Tom Oberg, Dave Costa, Floyd Little, Jerry Inman, Frank Richter, Carl Cunningham, John Huard, Equipment Manager Larry Elliott. Second row — Tommy Luke, Eric Crabtree, Fred Forsberg, Pete Duranko, Larry Kaminski, George Goeddeke, Bob Young, Curley Culp, Ron Lamb, Chip Myrtle. Third row — Assistant Coach Stan Jones, Head Coach Lou Saban, Marlin Briscoe, Gus Holloman, Terry Erwin, John McCormick, Jack Lentz, Jim Leclair, Charles Greer, Drake Garrett, Louri Green, Harold Lewis, Assistant Coach Sam Rutigliano, Assistant Coach Hunter Enis, Trainer Allen Hurst. Fourth row — Personnel Director Fred Gehrke, Bobby Moten, Robert Vaughn, Bob Humphreys, Sam Brunelli, Mike Haffner, Tom Cichowski, Wallace Dickey, Joe DiVito, Alex Moore, Dave Washington, Fran Lynch, Rich Jackson, Assistant Coach Whitey Dovell. Fifth row — Garrett Ford, Mike Current, Larry Cox, George Gaiser, Paul Smith, Tom Beer, Walter Highsmith, Gordon Lambert, Rex Mirich, Steve Tensi, Hubbard Lindsey, Assistant Equipment Manager Ronnie Bill.

PRE-SEASON (2-3-0)

15	Cincinnati 13
16	Minnesota 39
6	San Francisco 22
6	San Diego 3 (San Antonio)
7	Oakland 32 (Portland)

REGULAR SEASON (5-9-0)

10	at Cincinnati 24
2	at Kansas City 34
17	Boston 20
10	Cincinnati 7
21	at New York 13
24	at San Diego 55
21	Miami 14
35	at Boston 14
7	Oakland 43
17	at Houston 38
34	Buffalo 32
23	San Diego 47
27	at Oakland 33
7	Kansas City 30

Most yards interceptions returned:

        143 — Nemiah Wilson, 1967

Most touchdowns scored:

        13 — Floyd Little, 1973, 1972
        12 — Otis Armstrong, 1974
        12 — Lionel Taylor, 1960

Most extra points attempted:

        40 — Jim Turner, 1973

Most extra points made: 40 — Jim Turner, 1973

Most field goals attempted:

        39 — Gene Mingo, 1962

Most field goals made: 27 — Gene Mingo, 1962

Most points scored: 137 — Gene Mingo, 1962

INDIVIDUAL RECORDS • SINGLE GAME

Most rushing and passing plays:

        56 — Mickey Slaughter, vs. Houston, 12/20/64
        56 — Frank Tripucka, vs. Buffalo, 9/15/62

Most yards gained: 447 — Frank Tripucka, vs. Buffalo, 9/15/62
        445 — Charley Johnson, vs. Kansas City, 11/18/74

Most times carried ball: 32 — Cookie Gilchrist, vs. Boston, 9/24/65
        31 — Otis Armstrong, vs. Houston, 12/8/74

Most yards gained, rushing:

        183 — Otis Armstrong, vs. Houston, 12/8/74
        166 — Floyd Little, vs. Cincinnati, 10/19/69

Longest scoring run: 82 — Gene Mingo, vs. Oakland, 10/5/62
        80 — Floyd Little, vs. San Francisco, 10/25/70

Longest non-scoring run:

        68 — Henry Bell, vs. Los Angeles, 10/16/60
        63 — Jim Krieg, vs. San Diego, 12/10/72

Most passes attempted: 56 — Frank Tripucka, vs. Buffalo, 9/15/62
        53 — Mickey Slaughter, vs. Houston, 12/20/64

Most passes completed: 34 — Mickey Slaughter, vs. Houston, 12/20/64
        30 — Frank Tripucka, vs. Houston, 11/6/60

Most passes intercepted:

        6 — Don Horn, vs. Green Bay, 9/26/71
        6 — George Herring, vs. Houston, 11/26/61

Most yards passing: 447 — Frank Tripucka, vs. Buffalo, 9/15/62
        445 — Charley Johnson, vs. Kansas City, 11/18/74

1969 DENVER BRONCOS

Front row (left to right) — Al Denson, Rich Jackson, Tom Beer, Larry Kaminski, Floyd Little, Dave Costa, Sam Brunelli, Jerry Inman, Carl Cunningham, John Huard. Second row — Assistant Coach Dick MacPherson, Pete Liske, Pete Jaquess, Mike Current, Bob Young, Pete Duranko, Frank Richter, Wallace Dickey, Jay Bachman, Gordon Lambert, Fran Lynch, Personnel Director Fred Gehrke. Third row — Assistant Coach Whitey Dovell, General Manager and Head Coach Lou Saban, Bill Van Heusen, Phil Brady, Bobby Burnett, Jim Paul, Bruce Weinstein, Herman Lewis, Paul Smith, Garrett Ford, Mike Haffner, Steve Tensi, Assistant Coach Joe Collier, Assistant Coach Stan Jones. Fourth row — Assistant Coach Hunter Enis, Larry Cox, Grady Cavness, George Burrell, Al Pastrana, Mike Tomasini, Mike Schnitker, Bobby Howfield, Wes Plummer, Ed Hayes, Ken Criter, Bob Jackson, Tom Smiley, Assistant Coach Sam Rutigliano. Fifth row — Trainer Allen Hurst, Jimmy Smith, Bill Thompson, Drake Garrett, Wandy Williams, Rex Mirich, Henry Jones, Gary Crane, Gus Holloman, John Embree, Tom Oberg, Frank Quayle, Walter Highsmith, Equipment Manager Larry Elliott.

PRE-SEASON (1-4-0)

6 at Minnesota 26
22 New Orleans 28
19 San Francisco 15
10 Boston 26 (Jacksonville)
11 at Cincinnati 13

REGULAR SEASON (5-8-1)

26 Boston 21
21 New York 19
28 at Buffalo 41
13 Kansas City 26
14 Oakland 24
30 at Cincinnati 23
21 at Houston 24
13 San Diego 0
10 at Oakland 41
20 Houston 20
24 at San Diego 45
17 at Kansas City 31
24 at Miami 27
27 Cincinnati 16

Most touchdown passes:
> 5 — Frank Tripucka, vs. Buffalo, 10/28/62

Most consecutive games with TD pass:
> 10 — Charley Johnson (last 8 games of '73, first 2 games of '74)

Most consecutive completions:
> 11 — Steve Tensi, vs. San Diego, 11/23/69
> 10 — Frank Tripucka, vs. Dallas, 10/8/61

Longest scoring pass:
> 97 — George Shaw to Jerry Tarr, vs. Boston, 9/21/62
> 96 — Frank Tripucka to Al Frazier, vs. Buffalo, 9/15/62

Longest non-scoring pass:
> 74 — Don Horn to Floyd Little, vs. Oakland, 10/10/71
> 74 — Pete Liske to Bill Van Heusen, vs. New Orleans, 11/22/70

Most pass receptions:
> 13 — Bobby Anderson, vs. Chicago, 9/30/73
> 13 — Lionel Taylor, vs. Oakland, 11/29/64

Most yards gained on receptions:
> 199 — Lionel Taylor, vs. Buffalo, 11/27/60
> 172 — Lionel Taylor, vs. Buffalo, 9/19/65

Most touchdown receptions:
> 3 — Haven Moses, vs. Houston, 10/14/73
> 3 — Bob Scarpitto, vs. Buffalo, 12/18/66
> 3 — Lionel Taylor, vs. Buffalo, 11/27/60

Most punts:
> 12 — Bill Van Heusen, vs. Cincinnati, 10/6/68
> 12 — Bob Scarpitto, vs. Oakland, 9/19/67

Longest punt:
> 78 — Bill Van Heusen, vs. Dallas, 12/2/73
> 75 — Jim Fraser, vs. Oakland, 10/14/62

Most punt returns:
> 7 — Bill Thompson, vs. Kansas City, 10/6/74
> 6 — Four players tied

Most yards, punt returns:
> 103 — Bill Thompson, vs. Kansas City, 10/6/74
> 102 — Floyd Little, vs. New York Jets, 12/3/67

Longest scoring punt return:
> 76 — Gene Mingo, vs. Boston, 9/9/60
> 72 — Floyd Little, vs. New York Jets, 12/3/67

Longest non-scoring punt return:
> 60 — Bill Thompson, vs. Baltimore, 11/10/74
> 59 — Bill Thompson, vs. New England, 12/17/72

Most kickoff returns:
> 7 — Odell Barry, vs. Kansas City, 11/1/64
> 6 — Randy Montgomery, vs. San Diego, 9/24/72

Most yards, kickoff returns:
> 201 — Randy Montgomery, vs. San Diego, 9/24/72
> 185 — Floyd Little, vs. Miami, 9/17/67

1970

1970 DENVER BRONCOS

Front row (left to right) — Linebacker Coach Dick MacPherson, Al Denson, Jay Bachman, Steve Tensi, Sam Brunelli, Floyd Little, Dave Costa, Bob Young, Jerry Inman, George Goeddeke, Pete Duranko, Larry Kaminski, Equipment Manager Larry Elliott. Second row — General Manager and Head Coach Lou Saban, Billy Masters, Rich Jackson, Fran Lynch, Cornell Gordon, Mike Current, Booker Edgerson, Mike Haffner, Pete Jaquess, Fred Forsberg, Carl Cunningham, Mike Schnitker, Willis Crenshaw, Chip Myrtle, Walter Barnes. Third row — Personnel Director Fred Gehrke, Bill McKoy, Paul Smith, Charles Gogolak, Bill Van Heusen, George Saimes, Pete Liske, Charles Greer, Paul Martha, Bobby Howfield, Bob Anderson, Dick Davis, Defensive Backfield Coach Joe Collier, Offensive Line Coach Whitey Dovell, Offensive Backfield Coach Hunter Enis, Receiver Coach Sam Rutigliano, Trainer Allen Hurst. Fourth row — Defensive Line Coach Stan Jones, Randy Cayce, Alden Roche, Wandy Williams, Al Pastrana, Ken Criter, Drake Garrett, Rex Mirich, Bill Thompson, Dave Washington, John Embree, Bill Butler, Steve Alexakos, John Mosier, Jerry Hendren, Assistant Equipment Manager Ronnie Bill, Assistant Trainer Gene Bradshaw.

PRE-SEASON (3-2-0)

26 St. Louis 16
7 Baltimore 24
7 San Francisco 23 (Eugene, Ore.)
30 Chicago 17
16 Boston 14 (Salt Lake City)

REGULAR SEASON (5-8-1)

25 at Buffalo 10
16 Pittsburgh 13
26 Kansas City 13
23 at Oakland 35
24 Atlanta 10
14 at San Francisco 19
3 Washington 19
21 at San Diego 24
19 Oakland 24
31 at New Orleans 6
21 at Houston 31
0 at Kansas City 16
17 San Diego 17
13 Cleveland 27

208

Longest scoring kickoff return:
    100 — Goldie Sellers, vs. Houston, 10/2/66
    100 — Nemiah Wilson, vs. Kansas City, 10/8/66

Longest non-scoring kickoff return:
    89 — Floyd Little, vs. Oakland, 11/10/68
    88 — Randy Montgomery, vs. Oakland, 10/22/72

Longest scoring fumble return:
    80 — Bill Thompson, vs. Oakland, 10/22/73
    69 — Bud McFadin, vs. New York, 11/22/62

Most passes intercepted:
    4 — Willie Brown, vs. New York, 11/15/64
    4 — Goose Gonsoulin, vs. Buffalo, 9/18/60

Most yards interceptions returned:
    91 — Willie Brown, vs. New York, 11/15/64
    70 — Leroy Moore, vs. Boston, 11/20/64

Longest scoring interception return:
    70 — Nemiah Wilson, vs. Kansas City, 12/17/67
    65 — Nemiah Wilson, vs. San Diego, 11/7/65

Longest non-scoring interception return:
    70 — Leroy Moore, vs. Boston, 11/20/64
    65 — Buddy Alliston, vs. Buffalo, 9/18/60

Most touchdowns scored:
    3 — Otis Armstrong, vs. Houston, 12/8/74
    3 — Jon Keyworth, vs. Kansas City, 11/18/74
    3 — Haven Moses, vs. Houston, 10/14/73
    3 — Floyd Little, vs. Cincinnati, 9/16/73
    3 — Floyd Little, vs. Minnesota, 10/15/72
    3 — Bob Scarpitto, vs. Buffalo, 12/18/66
    3 — Don Stone, vs. San Diego, 11/4/62
    3 — Lionel Taylor, vs. Buffalo, 11/27/60

Most extra points attempted:
    6 — Jim Turner, vs. Houston, 10/14/73
    6 — Jim Turner, vs. New England, 12/17/72

Most extra points made:
    6 — Jim Turner, vs. Houston, 10/14/73
    6 — Jim Turner, vs. New England, 12/17/72

Most field goals attempted:
    7 — Gene Mingo, vs. San Diego, 10/6/63

Most field goals made: 5 — Gene Mingo, vs. San Diego, 10/6/63

Longest field goal: 53 — Bobby Howfield, vs. San Diego, 12/13/70
    53 — Gene Mingo, vs. San Diego, 9/7/62

Most points scored: 21 — Gene Mingo, vs. Los Angeles, 12/10/60
    20 — Bob Scarpitto, vs. Buffalo, 12/18/66
    20 — Gene Mingo, vs. San Diego, 10/6/63
    19 — Gene Mingo, vs. Oakland, 10/5/62
    18 — six players tied

1971 DENVER BRONCOS

Front row (left to right) — Director of Player Personnel Fred Gehrke, Equipment Manager Larry Elliott, Steve Ramsey, Jim Whalen, Bill Thompson, Floyd Little, Dave Costa, George Saimes, Larry Kaminski, Jerry Inman, Dick Post, Trainer Allen Hurst, Defensive Line Coach Stan Jones. Second row — Special Teams Coach Whitey Dovell, Offensive Line Coach Jerry Smith, Bob Anderson, Bill Van Heusen, Fran Lynch, Charles Greer, Sam Brunelli, Jay Bachman, Cornell Gordon, Paul Smith, Jim Turner, Larron Jackson, Mike Schnitker, Fred Forsberg, Chip Myrtle, Assistant Equipment Manager Ronnie Bill, Defensive Backfield Coach Joe Collier. Third row — Director of Scouting Carroll Hardy, Offensive Backfield Coach Hunter Enis, John Mosier, Billy Masters, Bob Geddes, Lyle Alzado, Randy Montgomery, Jerry Simmons, Jack Gehrke, Dwight Harrison, Pete Duranko, Ken Criter, Olen Underwood, Tommy Lyons, Clem Turner, Head Coach and General Manager Lou Saban, Assistant Trainer Dave Kendall, Team Physician Dr. Mack Clayton. Fourth row — Roger Shoals, Don Horn, Mike Current, Leroy Mitchell, Marv Montgomery, Butch Byrd, Dave Washington, Bill McKoy, Wandy Williams, Walt Barnes, George Goeddeke, Carter Campbell, Rich Jackson.

PRE-SEASON (1-4-0)

13 Washington 17
10 Atlanta 27 (Memphis)
17 San Francisco 33 (Stockton)
14 Minnesota 7
17 at Chicago 33

REGULAR SEASON (4-9-1)

10 Miami 10
13 at Green Bay 34 (Milwaukee)
3 Kansas City 16
16 Oakland 27
20 San Diego 16
27 at Cleveland 0
16 at Philadelphia 17
20 Detroit 24
10 Cincinnati 24
10 at Kansas City 28
22 at Pittsburgh 10
6 Chicago 3
17 at San Diego 45
13 at Oakland 21

OPPONENTS' RECORDS

Most points scored:	59 — Kansas City, 9/17/63
Most rushing and passing plays:	
	93 — Pittsburgh, 9/22/74 (OT)
	87 — Baltimore, 11/10/74
Most yards total offense:	634 — Oakland, 10/25/64
Most rushes:	52 — Chicago, 9/30/73
Most yards rushing:	380 — Kansas City, 10/23/66
Most passes attempted:	62 — New York, 12/3/67
Most passes completed:	31 — Pittsburgh, 9/22/74 (OT)
	25 — New York, 12/3/67
	25 — Oakland, 10/25/64
Most yards passing:	427 — Oakland, 10/25/64
Most touchdown passes:	6 — Kansas City, 11/1/64
Most first downs:	33 — Pittsburgh, 9/22/74 (OT)
	29 — Oakland, 10/25/64
	29 — Oakland, 12/17/60
Most first downs rushing:	16 — Pittsburgh, 9/22/74 (OT)
	16 — Houston, 11/12/67
Most first downs passing:	21 — San Diego, 12/1/68
Most first downs by penalties:	
	6 — Oakland, 11/9/69
	6 — Miami, 12/4/66
Most fumbles:	7 — Buffalo, 12/13/64
Most fumbles lost to Denver:	
	5 — Boston, 11/6/66
	5 — Buffalo, 12/13/64
	5 — Oakland, 10/14/62
Most penalties:	13 — Houston, 10/26/69
Fewest yards, total offense:	
	60 — Cleveland, 10/24/71
Fewest yards, rushing offense:	
	0 — Kansas City, 12/19/65
Fewest yards, passing offense:	
	−7 — Chicago, 12/5/71
Most rushing and passing plays:	
	60 — Joe Namath, New York, 12/3/67
Most yards gained:	448 — Len Dawson, Kansas City, 11/1/64
Most rushes:	27 — Abner Haynes, Dallas, 10/30/60
Most yards rushing:	183 — Paul Lowe, San Diego, 12/22/63
Longest scoring run:	69 — Curtis McClinton, Dallas, 12/9/62
Longest non-scoring run:	
	76 — Will Fowler, Buffalo, 11/27/60

1972 DENVER BRONCOS

Front row (left to right) — Bill Van Heusen, Randy Montgomery, Charley Johnson, Bill Thompson, Jerry Simmons, Fred Forsberg, Floyd Little, Paul Smith, Larry Kaminski, Steve Ramsey, Pete Duranko, George Saimes. Second row — Equipment Manager Larry Elliott, Mike Ernst, Lyle Alzado, Cornell Gordon, Leroy Mitchell, Bob Anderson, Marv Montgomery, Dwight Harrison, Larron Jackson, Jim Krieg, Mike Schnitker, Tom Domres, Rich Jackson, Chip Myrtle, Assistant Equipment Manager Ronnie Bill, Assistant General Manager Fred Gehrke. Third row — Chairman of the Board Gerald H. Phipps, Trainer Allen Hurst, Richard Wilkins, Riley Odoms, Tom Graham, Clem Turner, Joe Dawkins, Bill McKoy, Charles Greer, Bob Geddes, Bob Maples, Lloyd Voss, Jim Turner, Rod Sherman, Ken Criter, George Goeddeke, Assistant Trainer Dave Kendall, Allan Phipps. Fourth row — Head Coach and General Manager John Ralston, Linebacker Coach Bob Gambold, Defensive Line Coach Doc Urich, Defensive Coordinator Joe Collier, Billy Masters, John Mosier, Tony Harris, Fran Lynch, Mike Current, Don Horn, Mike Simone, Offensive Line Coach Jerry Frei, Wide Receiver Coach Dick Coury, Offensive Coordinator Max Coley, Special Teams Coach Myrel Moore.

PRE-SEASON (2-3-0)

0 at Washington 41
13 at St. Louis 17
27 at San Francisco 24
49 New England 24
13 Baltimore 20

REGULAR SEASON (5-9-0)

30 Houston 17
14 at San Diego 37
24 Kansas City 45
10 at Cincinnati 21
20 Minnesota 23
30 at Oakland 23
20 Cleveland 27
17 at N.Y. Giants 29
16 at Los Angeles 10
20 Oakland 37
20 at Atlanta 23
21 at Kansas City 24
38 San Diego 13
45 New England 21

Most passes attempted:	60 — Joe Namath, New York, 12/3/67
Most passes completed:	31 — Joe Gilliam, Pittsburgh, 9/22/74 (OT)
	24 — Joe Namath, New York, 12/3/67
	24 — George Blanda, Houston, 10/21/62
Most passes intercepted:	6 — Babe Parilli, Boston, 9/3/67
	6 — George Blanda, Houston, 11/14/65
Most yards passing:	435 — Len Dawson, Kansas City, 11/1/64
Most touchdown passes:	
	6 — Len Dawson, Kansas City, 11/1/64
Longest scoring pass play:	
	92 — Len Dawson to Tom Brooker, Dallas, 11/18/62
	92 — Jacky Lee to Bill Groman, Houston, 11/20/60
Longest non-scoring pass play:	
	77 — Tom Flores to Art Powell, Oakland, 11/29/64
Most pass receptions:	12 — Ed Podolak, Kansas City, 10/7/73
	12 — Art Powell, New York, 10/22/61
Most touchdown receptions:	
	4 — Lance Alworth, San Diego, 12/1/68
Longest punt:	98 — Steve O'Neal, New York, 9/21/69
Most punt returns:	9 — Roger Bird, Oakland, 9/10/67
Longest scoring punt return:	
	82 — Bobby Jancik, Houston, 12/20/64
Longest non-scoring punt return:	
	72 — Greg Pruitt, Cleveland, 10/27/74
Longest scoring kickoff return:	
	106 — Noland Smith, Kansas City, 12/17/67
Longest non-scoring kickoff return:	
	80 — Dave Grayson, Kansas City, 10/11/64
Longest scoring interception return:	
	80 — Coy Bacon, San Diego, 11/11/73
Longest non-scoring interception return:	
	87 — Ron Hall, Boston, 9/18/66
Most touchdowns:	4 — Lance Alworth, San Diego, 12/1/68
	4 — Bert Coan, Kansas City, 10/23/66
	4 — Frank Jackson, Dallas, 12/10/61
Most field goals:	6 — Gino Cappelletti, Boston, 10/4/64
Longest field goal:	57 — Don Cockroft, Cleveland, 10/29/72
Most points:	24 — Lance Alworth, San Diego, 12/1/68
	24 — Bert Coan, Kansas City, 10/23/66
	24 — Frank Jackson, Dallas, 12/10/61

1973

1973 DENVER BRONCOS

Front row (left to right) — Assistant Equipment Manager Ronnie Bill, Barney Chavous, Lyle Blackwood, Calvin Jones, Larry Kaminski, Bill Thompson, Charley Johnson, Floyd Little, Paul Smith, Jerry Inman, Lyle Alzado, Otis Armstrong, Ed Smith, Equipment Manager Larry Elliott. Second row — Chairman of the Board Gerald H. Phipps, Head Coach and General Manager John Ralston, Randy Montgomery, Charles Greer, Leroy Mitchell, Mike Simone, Fred Forsberg, Marv Montgomery, Larron Jackson, Tommy Lyons, Mike Current, Fran Lynch, Bill Van Heusen, Mike Ernst, Ken Criter, Haven Moses, Assistant General Manager Fred Gehrke, Corporate Secretary Richard S. Kitchen, Sr. Third row — Linebacker Coach Bob Gambold, Defensive Coordinator Joe Collier, Steve Ramsey, Bob Anderson, George Goeddeke, Mike Schnitker, Tom Domres, Dale Hackbart, Tom Graham, Pete Duranko, Jim Turner, John Hufnagel, Riley Odoms, John Grant, Jim O'Malley, Oliver Ross, Assistant Trainer Dave Kendall. Fourth row — Defensive Line Coach Doc Urich, Trainer Allen Hurst, Don Parish, Tom Jackson, Mike Askea, Billy Masters, Gene Washington, Paul Howard, Bill Laskey, Joe Dawkins, Jeff Baker, Bobby Maples, Jerry Simmons, Offensive Line Coach Jerry Frei,

PRE-SEASON (2-3-0)

10 at Washington 14
38 St. Louis 17
7 at San Francisco 43
16 Buffalo 14
10 Baltimore 17

REGULAR SEASON (7-5-2)

28 Cincinnati 10
34 San Francisco 36
14 Chicago 33
14 at Kansas City 16
48 at Houston 20
23 Oakland 23
40 at N.Y. Jets 28
17 at St. Louis 17
30 San Diego 19
23 at Pittsburgh 13
14 Kansas City 10
10 Dallas 22
42 at San Diego 28
17 at Oakland 21

RECORDS BY BOTH TEAMS

Most yards total offense: 1057 — Denver 476, San Diego 581, 10/20/68

Fewest yards total offense:
262 — Denver 102, Oakland 160, 11/20/66

Most yards passing: 708 — Denver 321, San Diego 387, 10/20/68

Most passes attempted: 97 — Denver 53, Houston 44, 12/2/62

Most passes completed: 53 — Denver 35, Houston 18, 12/20/64

Most passes intercepted:
13 — Denver 8, Houston 5, 12/2/62

Most touchdown passes: 8 — Denver 3, San Diego 5, 12/1/68
8 — Denver 3, San Diego 5, 10/20/68
8 — Denver 2, Kansas City 6, 11/1/64
8 — Denver 3, San Diego 5, 11/22/62

Fewest passing yards: 47 — Denver 54, Chicago −7, 12/5/71

Most rushing plays: 80 — Denver 43, Detroit 37, 11/7/71
80 — Denver 47, Kansas City 33, 10/10/65
80 — Denver 31, Buffalo 49, 11/27/60
80 — Denver 46, New York 34, 9/23/60

Most yards rushing: 431 — Denver 203, Detroit 228, 11/7/71

Fewest yards rushing: 91 — Denver 39, Houston 52, 12/2/67

Most fumbles: 12 — Denver 6, Boston 6, 11/6/66
12 — Denver 5, Buffalo 7, 12/13/64

Most fumbles lost: 10 — Denver 5, Boston 5, 11/6/66

Most yards penalized: 201 — Denver 90, Oakland 111, 11/29/64

Fewest yards penalized: 25 — Denver 5, Dallas 20, 10/30/60

Most first downs: 58 — Denver 34, Kansas City 24, 11/18/74
53 — Denver 20, Pittsburgh 33, 9/22/74 (OT)

Fewest first downs: 15 — Denver 7, Kansas City 8, 12/6/70

Most plays: 160 — Denver 67, Pittsburgh 93, 9/22/74 (OT)

Most yards gained: 1,057 — Denver 476, San Diego 581, 10/20/68

Most rushing plays: 80 — Denver 43, Detroit 37, 11/7/71
150 — Denver 76, Buffalo 74, 11/27/60

Most points scored: 91 — Denver 45, New York 46, 11/22/62

Fewest points scored: 9 — Denver 6, Chicago 3, 12/5/71

1974

1974 DENVER BRONCOS

Front row (left to right) — Assistant Equipment Manager Ronnie Bill, Oliver Ross, Bill Van Heusen, Jeff Baker, Calvin Jones, Bill Thompson, Floyd Little, Charley Johnson, Paul Smith, Lyle Alzado, Ozell Collier, Bob Anderson, John Grant. Second row — Defensive Line Coach Doc Urich, Chairman of the Board Gerald Phipps, Head Coach and General Manager John Ralston, Maurice Tyler, Charles Greer, John Hufnagel, Otis Armstrong, Fran Lynch, Bill Laskey, Jerry Simmons, Tom Lyons, Bobby Maples, Steve Ramsey, Tom Humphrey, Mike Schnitker, Al Barnes, John Rowser, Tom Jackson, Ed Smith, President Allan Phipps. Third row — Wide Receiver Coach Kay Dalton, Defensive Coordinator Joe Collier, Mike Askea, LeFrancis Arnold, Marv Montgomery, Larron Jackson, Joe Rizzo, Jon Keyworth, Randy Gradishar, Boyd Brown, Mike Current, Billy Masters, Pete Duranko, Mike Simone, Marv Frazier, John Pitts, Otto Stowe, Assistant General Manager Fred Gehrke, Trainer Allen Hurst, Equipment Manager Larry Elliott. Top row — Defensive Backfield Coach Bob Gambold, Larry Steel, Lonnie Hepburn, Charlie Johnson, Barney Chavous, Haven Moses, Cephus Weatherspoon, Riley Odoms, Ray May, Jim Turner, Carl Wafer, Paul Howard, Tom Graham, Jim O'Malley, Claudie Minor, Tom Drougas, Ken Criter, Offensive Line Coach Jerry Frei, Special Teams Coach Myrel Moore, Assistant Trainer Dave Kendall, Offensive Coordinator and Backfield Coach Max Coley.

BRONCOS' 1975 SCHEDULE

PRE-SEASON (2-4-0)	REGULAR SEASON (7-6-1)	PRE-SEASON	REGULAR SEASON
19 New York Jets 41	10 Los Angeles 17	Baltimore	Kansas City
27 Minnesota 21	35 Pittsburgh 35	New Orleans	Green Bay
10 San Francisco 3	3 at Washington 30	Houston	at Buffalo
31 at Green Bay 21	17 at Kansas City 14	at Chicago	at Pittsburgh
27 New England 21 (Spokane)	33 New Orleans 17	at San Francisco	Cleveland
14 Atlanta 20	27 San Diego 7	St. Louis	at Kansas City
	21 at Cleveland 23		Oakland
	17 Oakland 28		Cincinnati
	17 at Baltimore 6		at San Diego
	34 Kansas City 42		at Atlanta
	20 at Oakland 17		San Diego
	31 at Detroit 27		at Oakland
	37 Houston 24		Philadelphia
	0 at San Diego 17		at Miami

BRONCO ALL-TIME ROSTER

Player	Position	College	Years
ADAMSON, Kenneth	G	Notre Dame	1960-62
ALEXAKOS, Steve	G	San Jose State	1970
ALFLEN, Ted	RB	Springfield	1969
ALLEN, Buddy	HB	Utah State	1961
ALLEN, Donald	FB	Texas	1960
ALLISTON, Vaughn	LB	Mississippi	1960
ALZADO, Lyle	DE	Yankton	1971-73
AMES, David	HB	Richmond	1961
ANDERSON, Bobby	HB	Colorado	1970-73
ANDRUS, Lou	LB	Brigham Young	1967
ARMSTRONG, Otis	RB	Purdue	1973
ASKEA, Mike	T	Stanford	1973
ATKINS, Billy	DB	Auburn	1964
ATKINSON, Frank	DE	Stanford	1964
BACHMAN, Jay	C	Cincinnati	1968-71
BAKER, Jeff	WR	San Diego State	1973
BARNES, Ernie	G	North Carolina	1963-64
BARNES, Walter	DE	Nebraska	1969-71
BARRY, Odell	HB	Findlay	1964-65
BARTON, James	C	Marshall	1961-62
BASS, Norman	DB	University of Pacific	1964
BEER, Tom	OE	Houston	1967-69
BEHRMAN, Dave	C	Michigan State	1967
BELL, Henry	HB	None	1960
BERNARDI, Frank	HB	Colorado	1960
BERNET, Lee	OT	Wisconsin	1965-66
BOWDELL, Gordon	WR	Michigan State	1971
BRADY, Phil	S	Brigham Young	1969
BRAMLETT, John	LB	Memphis State	1965-66
BREAUX, Don	QB	McNeese State	1963
BREITENSTEIN, Bob	OT	Tulsa	1965-67
BRISCOE, Marlin	QB	Omaha	1968
BRODNAX, John	FB	Louisiana State	1960
BROWN, Hardy	LB	Tulsa	1960
BROWN, Willie	DB	Grambling	1963-66
BRUNELLI, Sam	G	Colorado State	1966-71
BUCKMAN, Tom	TE	Texas A&M	1969
BUKATY, Fred	FB	Kansas	1961
BURNETT, Bobby	RB	Arkansas	1969
BURRELL, George	S	Pennsylvania	1969
BUSSELL, Gerry	DB	Georgia Tech	1965
BUTLER, Bill	LB	San Fernando Valley	1970
BYRD, Butch	DB	Boston	1971
CAMPBELL, Carter	DE	Weber State	1971
CARMICHAEL, Albert	HB	Southern California	1960-61
CARMICHAEL, Paul	HB	El Camino JC	1965
CAROTHERS, Don	OE	Bradley	1960
CARPENTER, Kenneth	E	Oregon State	1960
CASEY, Tim	LB	Oregon	1969
CASH, John	E	Allen	1961-62
CASSESE, Tom	DB	C.W. Post	1967
CAVNESS, Grady	CB	Texas — El Paso	1969
CHAVOUS, Barney	DE	South Carolina State	1973
CHOBOIAN, Max	QB	San Fernando State	1966

218

Player	Position	College	Years
CICHOWSKI, Tom	OT	Maryland	1967-68
COFFEY, Don	E	Memphis State	1963
COOKE, Ed	E	Maryland	1964-65
COSTA, Dave	DT	Utah	1967-71
COTTRELL, Bill	G	Delaware Valley	1972
COX, Larry	DT	Abilene Christian	1966-68
CRABTREE, Eric	FL	Pittsburgh	1966-68
CRANE, Gary	LB	Arkansas State	1969
CRENSHAW, Willis	FB	Kansas State	1970
CRITER, Ken	LB	Wisconsin	1969-73
CUMMINGS, Ed	LB	Stanford	1965
CUNNINGHAM, Carl	LB	Houston	1967-70
CURRENT, Mike	OT	Ohio State	1967-73
DANENHAUER, Eldon	T	Kansas State Teachers	1960-65
DANENHAUER, William	E	Kansas State Teachers	1960
DAVIS, Dick	RB	Nebraska	1970
DAVIS, Jack	T	Arizona	1960
DAVIS, Marvin	DT	Wichita State	1966
DAWKINS, Joe	RB	Wisconsin	1971-73
DAY, Albert	T	Eastern Michigan	1960
DENSON, Al	FL	Florida A&M	1964-70
DENVIR, John	G	Colorado	1962
DICKEY, Wallace	OT	S.W. Texas State	1968-69
DICKINSON, Bo	FB	Southern Mississippi	1962-63
DIXON, Hewritt	HB-E	Florida A&M	1963-65
DiVITO, Joe	QB	Boston College	1968
DOMRES, Tom	DT	Wisconsin	1971-73
DOYLE, Skip	HB	Ohio State	1960
DUNCAN, Rick	K	Eastern Montana	1967
DURANKO, Pete	DE	Notre Dame	1967-73
EDGERSON, Booker	CB	Western Illinois	1970
ELFRID, Jim	LB	Colorado State	1961
EMBREE, John	WR	Compton JC	1969-70
ENIS, George	QB	Texas Christian	1962
EPPERSON, John	E	Adams State	1960
ERLANDSON, Thomas	LB	Washington State	1962-65
ERNST, Mike	QB	Cal – Fullerton	1972
ERWIN, Terry	HB	Boston College	1968
EVANS, Jay	HB	Kansas	1961
FANNING, Stan	E	Idaho	1964
FARR, Miller	DB	Wichita State	1965
FLETCHER, Billy	OE	Memphis State	1966
FORD, Garrett	FB	West Virginia	1968
FORSBERG, Fred	LB	Washington	1968-73
FRANCI, Jason	OE	Santa Barbara	1966
FRASER, Jim	LB	Wisconsin	1962-64
FRAZIER, Al	HB	Florida A&M	1961-63
FRAZIER, Marv	WR	Cheyney State	1973
GAISER, George	OT	SMU	1968
GAITERS, Bob	HB	New Mexico State	1963
GARRETT, Drake	DB	Michigan State	1968-70
GAVIN, Charles	E	Tennessee State	1960-63
GEDDES, Bob	LB	UCLA	1972
GEHRKE, Jack	WR	Utah	1971
GILCHRIST, Cookie	FB	None	1965-67
GLACKEN, Scotty	QB	Duke	1966-67
GLASS, Glenn	DB	Tennessee	1966
GOEDDEKE, George	G	Notre Dame	1967-73
GONSOULIN, Goose	DB	Baylor	1960-66

219

Player	Position	College	Years
GONZAGA, John	G	None	1966
GORDEN, Cornell	CB	North Carolina A&T	1970-72
GRAHAM, Tom	LB	Oregon	1972-73
GRANT, John	DE	Southern California	1973
GREER, Charles	DB	Colorado	1968-73
GREER, James D.	E	Elizabeth, N.C. State	1960
GRIFFIN, John	HB	Memphis State	1964-66
GROMAN, Bill	HB-E	Heidelberg	1963
GUESMAN, Dick	T	West Virginia	1964
GULSETH, Donald	LB	North Dakota	1966
GUY, Melwood	G	Duke	1961-62
HACKBART, Dale	S	Wisconsin	1973
HAFFNER, Mike	OE	UCLA	1968-70
HARRIS, Tony	WR	Toledo	1972
HARRISON, Dwight	WR	Texas A&I	1971-72
HATLEY, Johnny	T	Sul Ross State	1960
HAUSER, Arthur	T	Xavier	1961
HAYES, Wendell	HB	Humboldt State	1965-67
HAYNES, Abner	HB	North Texas State	1965-66
HENDREN, Jerry	WR	Idaho	1970
HENSON, Gary	E	Colorado	1964
HERRING, George	QB	Southern Mississippi	1960-61
HICKEY, Bo	FB	Maryland	1967
HIGHSMITH, Walter	C	Florida A&M	1968-69
HILL, Jack	HB	Utah State	1961
HOFFMAN, John	DE	Hawaii	1972
HOHMAN, Jon	G	Wisconsin	1965-66
HOLLOMAN, Gus	DB	Houston	1968-69
HOLZ, Gordon	T	Minnesota	1960-63
HOPKINS, Jerry	LB	Texas A&M	1963-66
HORN, Don	QB	San Diego State	1971-72
HOWARD, Paul	G	Brigham Young	1973
HOWFIELD, Bobby	K	None	1968-70
HUARD, John	LB	Maine	1967-69
HUDSON, Robert	LB	Clemson	1960-61
HUFNAGEL, John	QB	Penn State	1973
HUMPHREY, Tom	T	Abilene Christian	1973
HUMPHREYS, Bob	K	Wichita State	1967-68
INMAN, Jerry	DT	Oregon	1966-73
JACKSON, Larron	G	Missouri	1971-73
JACKSON, Richard	DE	Southern	1967-72
JACKSON, Tom	LB	Louisville	1973
JACKUNAS, Frank	C	Detroit	1963
JACOBS, Ray	T	Howard Payne	1963-66
JANERETTE, Charlie	T	Penn State	1964-65
JANIK, Tom	HB	Texas A&I	1963-64
JAQUESS, Pete	DB	Eastern New Mexico	1967-70
JESSUP, William	E	Southern California	1960
JETER, Eugene	LB	Arkansas A&M	1965-67
JOE, Billy	FB	Villanova	1963-64
JOHNSON, Charley	QB	New Mexico State	1972-73
JONES, Calvin	CB	Washington	1973
JONES, Henry	RB	Grambling	1969
JONES, Jimmy	OE	Wisconsin	1968
JORDAN, Larry	LB-E	Youngstown	1962-64
JOYCE, Donald	E	Tulane	1962
KAMINSKI, Larry	C	Purdue	1966-73
KEATING, Bill	DT	Michigan	1966-67
KELLOGG, Mike	FB	Santa Clara	1966-67

220

Player	Position	College	Years
KING, Donald	E	Kentucky	1960
KONOVSKY, Robert	E	Wisconsin	1961
KRIEG, Jim	WR	Washington	1972
KRONER, Gary	K	Wisconsin	1965-67
KUBALA, Ray	C	Texas A&M	1964-67
KUCHTA, Frank	C	Notre Dame	1960
LAMB, Ron	FB	South Carolina	1968
LAMBERT, Gordon	LB	Tennessee (Martin)	1968-69
LAMBERTI, Patsy	LB	Richmond	1961
LaROSE, Dan	DE	Missouri	1966
LARPENTER, Carl	G	Texas	1960-61
LASKEY, Bill	LB	Michigan	1973
LASSITER, Isaac	E	St. Augustine	1962-64
LECLAIR, Jim	QB	C.W. Post	1967-68
LECLERC, Roger	C	Trinity (Conn.)	1967
LEE, Jacky	QB	Cincinnati	1964-65
LEETZOW, Max	DE	Idaho	1965-66
LENTZ, Jack	DB	Holy Cross	1967-68
LESTER, Darrell	FB	McNeese State	1965-66
LEWIS, Herman	DE	Virginia Union	1968
LINDSEY, Hub	HB	Wyoming	1968
LISKE, Pete	QB	Penn State	1969-70
LITTLE, Floyd	HB	Syracuse	1967-73
LUKE, Tommy	LB	Mississippi	1968
LYNCH, Fran	HB	Hofstra	1967-73
LYONS, Tom	G	Georgia	1971-73
MANGUM, Pete	LB	Mississippi	1960
MAPLES, Bobby	C	Baylor	1972-73
MARSHALL, Charles	HB	Oregon State	1962
MARTHA, Paul	S	Pittsburgh	1970
MASTERS, Billy	TE	Louisiana State	1970-73
MATSON, Pat	G	Oregon	1966-67
MATSOS, Archie	LB	Michigan State	1966
MATTOX, Jack	T	Fresno State	1961-62
MATUSZAK, Marv	LB	Tulsa	1964
MAY, Ray	LB	Southern California	1973
McCARTHY, Brendan	FB	Boston College	1968-69
McCORMICK, John	QB	Massachusetts	1963, 65-6, 68
McCULLOUGH, Robert	G	Colorado	1962-65
McDANIEL, Wahoo	LB	Oklahoma	1961-63
McFADIN, Bud	T	Texas	1960-63
McGEEVER, John	HB	Auburn	1962-65
McKOY, Bill	LB	Purdue	1970-72
McMILLIN, James	HB	Colorado State	1960-62, 64-5
McNAMARA, Robert	HB	Minnesota	1960-61
MINGO, Gene	HB-K	None	1960-64
MINTER, Tommy	HB	Baylor	1962
MIRICH, Rex	DE	Northern Arizona	1967-69
MITCHELL, Alvin	WR-S	Morgan State	1970
MITCHELL, Charlie	HB	Washington	1963-67
MITCHELL, Leroy	CB	Texas Southern	1971-73
MONTGOMERY, Marv	T	Southern California	1971-73
MONTGOMERY, Randy	CB	Weber State	1971-73
MOORE, Alex	HB	Norfolk State	1968
MOORE, Leroy	E	Fort Valley (Ga.)	1964-65
MOSES, Haven	WR	San Diego State	1972-73
MOSIER, John	TE	Kansas	1971
MOTEN, Bobby	OE	Bishop College	1968
MYRTLE, Chip	LB	Maryland	1967-73

221

Player	Position	College	Years
NERY, Ron	E	Wisconsin	1963
NICHOLS, Mike	C	Arkansas A&M	1960-61
NOCERA, John	LB	Iowa	1963
NOMINA, Tom	G	Miami, Ohio	1963-65
NUGENT, Philip	HB	Tulane	1961
OBERG, Tom	DB	Portland State	1968-69
ODOMS, Riley	TE	Houston	1972-73
OLSON, Harold	T	Clemson	1963-64
OLSZEWSKI, John	FB	California	1962
O'MALLEY, Jim	LB	Notre Dame	1973
PARK, Ernie	G	McMurry	1967
PARKER, Charlie	G	Southern Mississippi	1965
PARISH, Don	LB	Stanford	1972
PASTRANA, Al	QB	Maryland	1969-70
PERKINS, James	T	Colorado	1962-64
PETE, Dennis	DB	San Francisco State	1972
PETERS, Anton	T	Florida	1963
PITTS, John	S	Arizona State	1973
PIVEC, Dave	TE	Notre Dame	1969
PLY, Bobby	DB	Baylor	1967
POST, Dickie	RB	Houston	1971
PREBOLA, Eugene	E	Boston	1961-63
PREECE, Steve	S	Oregon State	1972
PRICE, James	LB	Auburn	1964
PRISBY, Errol	DB	Cincinnati	1967
PYEATT, John	HB	None	1960
QUAYLE, Frank	RB	Virginia	1969
RAMSEY, Steve	QB	North Texas State	1971-73
REED, Leo	T	Colorado State	1961
RICHARDSON, Bob	DB	UCLA	1966
RICHTER, Frank	LB	Georgia	1967-69
ROCHE, Alden	DE	Southern Illinois	1970
ROEHNELT, William	LB	Bradley	1961-63
ROLLE, David	FB	Oklahoma	1960-61
ROMINE, Albert	HB	Florence State	1960
ROSS, Oliver	RB	Alabama A&M	1973
ROTE, Tobin	QB	Rice	1966
ROWLAND, Justin	HB	Texas Christian	1962
RYCHLEC, Tom	E	American International	1963
SAIMES, George	S	Michigan State	1970-73
SBRANTI, Ron	LB	Utah State	1966
SCARPITTO, Bob	FL	Notre Dame	1962-67
SCHNITKER, Mike	G	Colorado	1969-73
SCOTT, Lew	DB	Oregon State	1966
SEARS, James	HB	Southern California	1960-61
SELLERS, Goldie	DB	Grambling	1966-67
SHACKELFORD, Don	G	University of Pacific	1964
SHARP, Rick	T	Washington	1972
SHAW, George	QB	Oregon	1962
SHERMAN, Rod	WR	Southern California	1972
SHOALS, Roger	T	Maryland	1971
SIMMONS, Jerry	WR	Bethune-Cookman	1971-73
SIMMONS, Leon	LB	Grambling	1963
SIMONE, Mike	LB	Stanford	1972-73
SIMPSON, Jack	LB	Mississippi	1961
SKLOPAN, John	HB	Southern Mississippi	1963
SLAUGHTER, Mickey	QB	Louisiana Tech	1963-66
SMILEY, Tom	RB	Lamar Tech	1969
SMITH, Dan	HB	Northeast Oklahoma	1961

222

layer	Position	College	Years
MITH, Don	G	Florida A&M	1967
MITH, Ed	DE	Colorado College	1973
MITH, Harold	T	UCLA	1960
MITH, Hugh	E	Kansas	1962
MITH, James	S	Utah State	1969
MITH, Paul	DE	New Mexico	1968-73
MITH, Willie	G	Western Michigan	1960
NORTON, Matt	E	Michigan State	1964
ORRELL, Henry	LB	Chattanooga	1967
TALCUP, Jerry	LB	Wisconsin	1961-62
TARLING, Bruce	HB	Florida	1963
TINNETTE, James	FB-LB	Oregon State	1961-62
TOKES, Jesse	DB	Corpus Christi	1968
TONE, Don	FB	Arkansas	1961-64
TRANSKY, Robert	HB	Colorado	1960
TRICKLAND, David	T-G	Memphis State	1960
TURM, Jerry	C-T-G	Illinois	1961-66
UMMERS, Jim	DB	Michigan State	1967
WEENEY, Neal	OE	Tulsa	1967
YKES, Gene	DB	LSU	1967
ARASOVIC, George	DE	LSU	1967
ARR, Jerry	E	Oregon	1962
AYLOR, Lionel	E	New Mexico Highlands	1960-66
ENSI, Steve	QB	Florida State	1967-70
HIBERT, Jim	LB	Toledo	1965
HOMPSON, Bill	CB	Maryland State	1969-73
HOMPSON, Jim	DT	Southern Illinois	1965
OBEY, Dave	LB	Oregon	1968
RAYNHAM, Jerry	HB	Southern California	1961
RIPUCKA, Frank	QB	Notre Dame	1960-63
URNER, Clem	RB	Cincinnati	1970-72
URNER, Jim	K	Utah State	1971-73
YLER, Maurice	S	Morgan State	1973
YSON, Richard	G	Tulsa	1967
NDERWOOD, Olen	LB	Texas	1971
AN HEUSEN, Bill	WR-P	Maryland	1968-73
AUGHAN, Bob	G	Mississippi	1968
OSS, Lloyd	OT	Nebraska	1972
ADE, Bob	CB	Morgan State	1970
ALKER, Clarence	HB	Southern Illinois	1963
ASHINGTON, Dave	LB	Alcorn A&M	1971
ASHINGTON, Dave	OE	Southern California	1968
ASHINGTON, Gene	WR	Michigan State	1973
EGERT, Ted	FB	None	1961
EST, Bill	CB	Tennessee State	1972
EST, Willie	HB	Oregon	1964
ETTSTEIN, Max	OE	Florida State	1966
HALEN, Jim	TE	Boston College	1970-71
HITE, Andre	OE	Florida A&M	1967
ILLIAMS, Harold	HB	Miami, Ohio	1961
ILLIAMS, Wandy	RB	Hofstra	1969-70
ILSON, Nemiah	DB	Grambling	1965-67
OOD, Richard	QB	Auburn	1962
RIGHT, James	HB	Memphis State	1964
RIGHT, Lonnie	DB	Colorado State	1966-67
ELVERTON, William	E	Mississippi	1960
OUNG, Joseph	E	Arizona	1960-61
OUNG, Robert	G	Howard Payne	1966-70
EMAN, Robert	HB	Wisconsin	1962-63